Prai[illegible]

In the Meantime

"This timely and dynamic message has everything you need to transition successfully from one season to the next in your life. Its frank style will position, then equip and empower you. Rob Brendle is brilliant, fun, and witty. He is a man who has moved wisely within his years. Read *In the Meantime*...and reap."

—JOHN AND LISA BEVERE, speakers and authors of *Drawing Near* and *Kissed the Girls and Made Them Cry*

"Finally, a guide to help us do what most of us do so poorly—*wait!* Insightful, practical, and truly witty, Rob Brendle pens the heartfelt path from God's calling to the fulfillment of his call. Bravo!"

—DOUGLAS WEISS, PhD, executive director of Heart to Heart Counseling Center

"Rob Brendle's book is an important contribution for young people who are confused about the pursuit of God's will for their lives. It's also a great reminder for the not-so-young who need to continue on the journey with the Author who writes all of our stories for his grand plan. Rob has a gift for writing in both a humorous and down-to-earth style, and he clearly is one who is living his calling."

—ED YOUNG, senior pastor of Fellowship Church, Grapevine, Texas, and author of *YOU! The Journey to the Center of Your Worth*

"It's encouraging to know that someone as young as Rob Brendle has the kind of insight and wisdom that *In the Meantime* displays. If you're seeking God's purpose for your life, pursuing his vision, desiring a deeper relationship with him, and, most of all, wondering when it's all going to come together—this book offers a surprising depth of understanding that will aid you in your quest."

—THOMAS S. FORTSON, PHD, president/CEO,
Promise Keepers

"A young pastor brimming with zeal and wise beyond his years, Rob Brendle conveys a fine combination of Christian insight and earthly good sense in this stimulating, enjoyable book."

—DINESH D'SOUZA, fellow at the Hoover Institution,
Stanford University, and author of *What's So Great About America*

In the Meantime

the practice of proactive waiting

Rob Brendle

WATERBROOK
PRESS

IN THE MEANTIME
PUBLISHED BY WATERBROOK PRESS
12265 Oracle Boulevard, Suite 200
Colorado Springs, Colorado 80921
A division of Random House, Inc.

Italics in Scripture quotations reflect the author's added emphasis.

ISBN 1-4000-7008-2

Library of Congress Cataloging-in-Publication Data
Brendle, Robert.
In the meantime : the practice of proactive waiting / Robert Brendle.—1st ed.
p. cm.
Includes bibliographical references
ISBN 1-4000-7008-2
1. Expectation (Psychology)—Religious aspects—Christianity. 2. Trust in God. 3. Patience—Religious aspects—Christianity. 4. Christian life. I. Title.
BV4647.E93B74 2005
248.4—dc22 2005024388

Printed in the United States of America
2006—First Edition

10 9 8 7 6 5 4 3 2 1

Merry Christmas Garrett - 2009
from Grandma and Grandpa Slater
Love you so much!

■ ■ ■

To my mom and dad, Tom and Judy Brendle.
You trained me in the way I should go before I knew any better,
nurtured my calling before I valued it myself,
and tirelessly cheered on my writing.

Contents

Jesus said that He came to give His followers life—*abundant life.* What an incredible promise—that any of us, regardless of the experiences of the past or the circumstances of the present, can tap into a rich, deep, never-ending supply of Jesus's *life!*

At New Life Church, we encourage the flow of this Christ-energized life into every individual and endeavor. We challenge our staff to produce life-giving ideas, life-changing messages, and life-saving advice that will equip our people to embrace the fullness of God's promises in relationships, family, small groups, church, community, and even the world.

This desire to seize all the life Jesus promised is why we joined in partnership with WaterBrook Press to produce LifeGiving Books—high-quality publications that deliver a refreshing and empowering sip of the abundant living water Christ gives to those who earnestly seek and follow Him.

Welcome to another LifeGiving Book! God bless you as you read.

Here's to *Life!*

—PASTOR TED HAGGARD

New Life Church, Colorado Springs

Foreword

I think highly of Rob Brendle. If Rob were not one of the associate pastors at New Life Church, he would be the senior pastor of a booming mega-church, or the chief engineer of a major architectural firm in Manhattan, or at the cusp of a brilliant military service career. While doing any one of these things, he would probably be preparing to run for local political office on his way to a career in national public service. He might even be advocating an end to "age discrimination" so that he could run for president before turning thirty-five.

Rob is a visionary, and he has the goods. He's one of the most promising young Christian leaders I know. I say all this because I really want you to listen to Rob Brendle. Read this book carefully, and it will be a blessing to you. It will bring you comfort and wisdom. It will bring you hope. And it may even save you from despair and give you the keys to a life of success.

Rob wants you to know that God is using you for his purposes. And he is using you right now.

This book highlights the difference between fulfilling your calling and establishing a career path while pursuing your calling. See the difference? God has called all of us to serve in his kingdom, and all of us have been called in specific and special ways that can be discovered *right now.* God is a masterful director, and the smallest details of our lives are pieces of his plan in ways that never occur to us—at least not until we learn to see them.

I was raised in a Christian culture that emphasized our calling in Christ, which was good. The unintended consequence of this emphasis, though, was that our Christian living took on the appearance of a Christian career path: We were always headed somewhere else. As a result, we often missed the opportunities of day-to-day life.

Then it dawned on me: God calls us to be faithful in the little opportunities that present themselves every day. If we will take advantage of those opportunities, we will make the decisions that set us up for what God desires for us tomorrow. Put days well lived together, and you have a decade of divine direction. Put several such decades together, and you have a calling fulfilled—all by living faithfully day by day.

When I was a youth pastor, I always had bright, articulate young people wanting to help me lead services. I never told them why, but I actually chose for leadership the ones who were serving—those who picked up trash, showed up to do the dirty work, loved and took care of others. I overlooked the ones who had worked out a career path to the platform. The one who helped the handicapped kid play baseball got the prize. I think God works something like that.

Rob also explains that God doesn't need to be convinced of our fitness or readiness to be used by him. Rob says we are "hard-wired" to serve God. The desire to love, know, and serve him is in the fiber of our being. The mystery is not whether he desires to have us work in his kingdom. The mystery is the variety of ways we prevent ourselves from simply doing so.

When Rob explained this idea, I realized that I'd never seen it articulated so crisply or convincingly. It was one of those "aha" moments when we hear an idea and realize it's something we've always believed but never heard put so perfectly. Then the full force of the notion hits us, and it becomes an idea that is permanently added to our lives. This happened to me over and over again while enjoying Rob's book—I found myself laughing, nodding in agreement, underlining whole passages.

Here's how I know Rob Brendle is a wise man: He understands the difference between "living" and "living into." That's one of my favorite phrases in this book: "living into the calling." Life is a journey, and even if we know what we want our destination to be—even if we know *exactly* who we want to marry or *exactly* what kind of work we want to do—we can't always see that result in the road just ahead. Sometimes God keeps us from arriving for a very good reason. Sometimes the path toward our calling *is in fact our calling.* The process of moving toward the calling is an important part of the calling itself.

Rob also articulates the value of this process—its "in the meantime" significance. While we are working toward God's destination for us, if we will see where we are today, we will realize that both our current situations and our eventual destinations have equal import. If we have questions, we can live into the answers. If we have been called, we can live into the calling. In the meantime, we can do life well, whatever is required of us.

According to Rob, we are never called in a bubble. This is a *huge* concept. We are not called in isolation. Instead, we are called within the context of history and relationships. We are called in the midst of the sovereign purpose God has for his body during our generation. Our story is a piece of the big story. Rob rightly highlights that God has a plan that will be fulfilled on the earth through the church in our generation, and by our submission to God, we are swept into that plan. The plan isn't about us, but rather it's about a global story that we can participate in through submission to Christ and membership in the church.

That's why pursuing God's plan for our lives in isolation from our churches will leave us in confusion and will potentially render us ineffective. Some of Rob's contemporaries are whining about the people of God and the work of God that disappoint them. Too many think they are being insightful when they identify weaknesses in others. Rob demonstrates his wisdom by showing the value of bypassing self-centeredness and living a life based on purpose rather than viewing everything from a self-oriented perspective. He grasps God's reality and says it straight: God doesn't call us in isolation. He calls us in the midst of his family. Outside of the church, we can't hope to find our purpose. But if we plunge into the life of a local body of believers, we have the opportunity to discover the fullness of God's plan for our lives—to "live into" our calling.

Rob says we have to wait, and that waiting is good. So we wait, and wait *well.*

And what do we do in the day-to-day? We serve and honor God with our lives. We humbly contribute. We make things better for others. We live as if this day is our last, but also as if we are on a journey into a brighter future. We practice obedience to the Scriptures. We practice living in love, joy, peace, patience, kindness, goodness, faithfulness, gentleness, and self-control. We need time for that practice. That's what today is for.

Rob expounds on all these ideas in these pages, and he does it wonderfully. His stories are funny and gripping, his insights profound. My only concern after putting the book down is that I wished it had been written twenty years ago. I have needed this book for a long time.

I can't think of a better way for Rob to "live into his calling" than to be a voice of wisdom in his generation. He would never say that about himself. (And if he believed it, it probably wouldn't be true!) But I'm his pastor and his friend. I can say it and believe it. May this be the first of many times that we hold a Rob Brendle book in our hands.

—TED HAGGARD

senior pastor, New Life Church

Acknowledgments

Thank you:

Mauri, Ellie, and Caden—for believing in me. You make me feel like a king.

Ted—for knowing when to be my pastor, when to be my mentor, and when to be my friend.

Justin and Gaby Spicer—you are the world's most faithful friends.

Bill Walton, my comrade in arms—for picking up the slack while I wrote.

Andrew Mondy—for all your help writing this book, and for doing everything else.

SATURDAYNIGHT—for giving me the opportunity to live into my calling.

New Life Church—for loving me like family.

Chapter 1

I Have a Dream...Do You?

> I say to you today, my friends, that in spite of the difficulties and frustrations of the moment, I still have a dream.
>
> —MARTIN LUTHER KING JR., August 28, 1963 at the Lincoln Memorial

We were two tall white boys and a short black man, and we walked along a dirt road in the midsummer heat. Matt and I were college students taking a summer to give something back. We were in the middle of East Africa, and we felt acutely out of place in every way. Our assignment was to shadow and serve an African pastor named Mbithi—a wonderful, godly man—and gain in the process an enlarged appreciation for what God was doing around the world.

Most of the time when we were shadowing Mbithi, he was walking. Now understand, there's putting on your slippers and walking to the end of the driveway to get the paper, there's putting on your sneakers at lunchtime and walking around the office complex, and then there's *walking*—very far, briskly, and in suffocating heat. Mbithi was the overseer of around twenty-five churches in villages outside the city of Kitui, Kenya, and one gets to those twenty-five or so surrounding villages just one way: walking. Consequently, Mbithi spent much of his time trekking from village to village, encouraging the believers in each church to stay faithful to God, to study the Scriptures, and to preach the gospel with boldness.

Mbithi was small in stature, but he had huge calves, and I suppose it was either those calves or his fierce love for those little churches that enabled him to walk long distances at such a torrid clip. Whatever it was, we walked and walked, and when about ten miles down the road he finally suggested we stop for a breather, there was no protesting from the American teenagers. I ambled off the side of the road and up a slight hill. I stood for a moment and gazed out over the East African plains, not really thinking anything beyond hoping the moleskin on my right heel would keep a blister from forming there. In the moment that followed, something amazing—something unforgettable—happened to me. I heard God for the first time in my life.

As I stood there looking out over the land, I sensed God speak to me. His voice was not audible, but it was unmistakable. Here is what he said: *You are not going to do the things you think you are going to do. You are going to serve me for the rest of your life, and you're going to love it.* Oooh…just typing these words makes me tingly. The message was so vivid, surreal, and transcendent, and its ending was so abrupt. Remember in *Star Wars* when Luke Skywalker was cleaning up R2-D2 in Uncle Owen's maintenance shop on Tatooine? He pried loose some bolt that was stuck, and all of a sudden, to his astonishment, the image of Princess Leia projected from R2 onto the dusty ground. In wide-eyed wonderment, Luke watched and listened as this beautiful, white-cloaked mystery woman spoke of the things of the galaxy and pleaded for his help. And then she was gone. With trademark pubescent flair, Luke protested the hologram's disappearance—but it was gone, and he was alone with his newly awakened destiny.

That's exactly how Africa was for me. "Wait a minute!" I remember saying aloud. "Come back! Tell me more! What am I supposed to *do?!*"

Now, twelve years later, I am more sure than ever that God spoke to me on the high plains of East Africa. Since that day I have viewed the world, made decisions, and navigated my life through the lens of that experience. Many times along the road during this past decade, I have been inclined to question the authenticity of God's call on my life and the dreams he has placed within me. Each time, my Damascus Road experience has proven to be a touch point, a reference mark for my faith. Even when it seemed as if God wasn't fulfilling his promise, I could return to this one, clear, faith-activating reality: I *know* that I heard God. I know that I know that I know. If for no other reason, I know that I heard God that day because of what has happened in my life since then. Truly, I am *not* doing what I thought I was going to do—far, far from it!—and I *am* serving God vocationally. Best of all, I am loving it!

I am a civil engineer by training, and engineering is a science. That is to say, it's not an art. In engineering, there is a right answer, and there is a wrong answer. You can go to the back of the textbook and find out whether the load distribution you calculated for a horizontal structural member is correct. (This, of course, is not the case with the arts, which is something I greatly enjoyed reminding my liberal, Marxist, feminist literature professors when they told me that my analysis was wrong and that Hamlet was, in fact, a frustrated bisexual who harbored a secret oedipal love for his mother.) I chose engineering as a discipline and thrived in that course of study because my mind works that way. Concrete concepts. Absolute answers.

You'd think it would follow, then, that I would need something more certain and tangible on which to hinge my life's direction. But in an ironic way, my African plains encounter has been my bedrock back-of-the-book answer for the past twelve years. Ironic because it was precisely nonprecise: not absolute or concrete or real to people in any of the ways I would have wanted. Bedrock because, however implausible a touch point in other people's eyes, it is more real to me than the chair I am sitting in as I type these words. As I have pondered this paradox over the years, a confidence has grown in me: If I can't prove I'm right, you can't tell me I'm wrong. I'm not the dumbest guy out there, I'm not given to sensationalism, and I'm fairly healthy emotionally—and *you can't tell me I'm wrong!*

My point is this: I never looked back. I heard the very voice of God, and that is enough. Now I know where I am going, if only a general direction. There are lots of cases to be tried, political offices to be won, and dollars to be earned, but they all pale when compared to the bright-shining call of God. I remember making this decision back in 1994: *I have a dream, and though I know not exactly where it will lead or precisely how it will unfold, I know with conviction that it is from God and that it can, will, must unfold. I have a dream, and I will never look back.*

Come on...you've been there, haven't you? God touched you on the shoulder one day and gave you a dream. Maybe you were on a desert road in East Africa following a short, large-calved man as he walked from one tribal village to another. Maybe you were repairing droids on Tatooine. Maybe you were seeking God passionately or maybe you were running from him or maybe you were just living out your life doing your best, and he came to you and it was irresistible.

Whatever happened, God caught hold of you. Maybe you had never heard his voice before or maybe you had been taught not to expect him to speak to you at all. Maybe you had followed him all your life and cultivated the ability to distill with laserlike precision the still small voice from the clamor of daily living. Maybe he furnished you with rich details of the promised land and a road map to get you there, or maybe, as he did with me, he gave you a nudge and a smile and vanished into thin air. However the scene played out, you believe that his call was real, you are zealous to fulfill your destiny in Christ, and you desperately want to hear from God to learn how to get there from here.

I remember returning to America at the end of that life-changing summer in Africa. After the obligatory week and a half of "cultural re-entry," I began to clearly see the road ahead. (In case you are new to summer missions, cultural re-entry is the period during which you feel righteous anger over the fact that there is one aisle in every American grocery store devoted entirely to chips, while people in the country from which you just returned still use an outhouse.) Yep, everything was different for me now. I was *called.* I would serve *him* now. I was going into the *ministry.* With a secret aloofness, I would smile knowingly and think of sitting through career fairs, appointments with the job-placement counselor, and find-your-true-purpose motivational speeches with the rest of the students for the next two years, confident that my destiny was sealed.

But here was the problem: I hadn't a clue how to proceed. So I was going to be in the ministry! Fantastic! The excitement of that prospect sustained me for a year or two, but eventually the dam cracked that had been holding back a flood of questions on the edge of my consciousness—and then the dam broke entirely. *What specifically will I do? How will I get there? How will I know I'm on the right path?* You know how it is: You start to look for a sign—a burning bush or an angelic visitation or a wet fleece. You spiritualize things: *Maybe the weed whacker getting tangled in the lawn decorations last weekend was God sending me a message; maybe he was speaking to me through the unusually crisp, minty-fresh feeling of the new toothpaste I bought.* You go through seasons when you feel God wildly; everything seems to be his leading, and the moment of embarking on your calling seems imminent. And you go through seasons when you feel absolutely nothing. You become sure that, like Moses and David before you, you are in The Desert, and you somberly resign yourself to the possibility that you may have to wander for years in order for God to teach you something. You sensationalize and rationalize and begin to drive yourself crazy, all in pursuit of this elusive sense of calling.

So the sublime self-assurance of my Damascus Road experience proved short-lived. If the sudden enlightenment I experienced that summer solved one problem, it created another. Now I no longer wondered what career discipline I would choose or whether I would pass the dreaded engineer-in-training exam, and if not, whether my life would end. But a whole new set of questions emerged. Questions about details, decisions, direction. It was all so hazy.

What exactly am I to do? "You will serve me for the rest of your life..." Does that mean I'll be a pastor in a church? What about a leader in a parachurch ministry? But alas, I was on the mission field when he called me, so maybe that means I'm supposed to be a missionary! That certainly qualifies as serving him, right? Ah, but then again, all believers in Christ are called to serve him, so technically he could have meant that I would have a normal career and be a light in the darkness of my workplace. So maybe I need to be studying for the dumb engineer-in-training exam after all! Oh c'mon, that's not what he meant! Why would he come and speak to me in The Desert when I was already serving him—according to this technicality—only to tell me the obvious? Okay, smarty, so what did he mean then?

In retrospect, I remind myself of Gollum in *The Two Towers* when he was having a prolonged conversation with himself. My internal wrangling was somewhat comical, but it sure wasn't funny at the time! No, these were the questions of the cosmos to my twenty-year-old mind. *I* will *serve you—yes, undoubtedly. But what are the steps to get there?* The voice sort of disappeared before we got to that part. Give me commands, and I can obey them exactly; give me a map, and I can follow it precisely. I can work hard, focus, and sacrifice. But the ambiguity of *"Serve me for the rest of your life"* threw me because God didn't provide any subsequent commands or give me a road map. I went to Africa full of naive ambitions and good-hearted, boyish dreams; I came home full of the big questions of life.

These questions shaped my young adulthood. The next twelve years became a process of finding the answers. Sometimes the answers came as a result of a deliberate search, and other times I stumbled onto them as I walked along the path God laid before me. I can see now that all the while I was living into the calling God gave me. I have become persuaded that these big questions are the stuff of the pursuit of God, that he intentionally places them within us. It is in living into the answers and seeing the plan unfold that men and women of substance are forged. Some people never get past the questions, and that is a shame, because theirs become wasted dreams of God.

Determined not to let my God-dream ferment, I set out to learn how to be used by God. You know how it goes. You wait on the Lord. You confess and believe you are called by God. Forgetting what is behind and straining toward what is ahead, you press on and pray hard and in dramatic goose-bump moments at the climax of powerful worship services, you cry out with all your might, "God, use me!" You pause, throw back your head, and then say it again, more passionately this time, drawing out the second syllable: "God, uuuuuse me!" Your uplifted hands tremble a little now as you fall to your knees and cry out once more, this time with a twinge of vibrato, "God, uuuuuuuuse meeeee!!"

■ ■ ■

This brings me to the point of this book. Over the past several years, I have come to believe that the sincerely meant and dramatically expressed petitions of my early adulthood were entirely off the mark. In fact, it's clear to me now that my pleas for God to use me were nonsensical, and here's why. Passionately pleading for God to use us is like passionately pleading for fire to be hot or for water to be wet. God by his very nature uses people. Yet we have cultivated for ourselves an unwritten theology that we must persuade God to use us to accomplish his plans. It's as if he were determined to use angels or seraphim or the perpetually bowing elders to build his kingdom, and we try to convince him with our passion and our logic and our sheer resolve to let us do it instead. So we imagine that we twist his arm until he cries uncle and finally says, "Oh, all right. Go ahead and do some work for my kingdom if you must." Friend, understand that serving God to advance his kingdom's dominion on the earth is not something we have to beg him to do; it's something he has already chosen for us. It is hard-wired into our very being to respond affirmatively to this choice of his. His call on our lives—the very call we have believed and cherished—confirms it.

Realizing this is at once reassuring and unsettling—reassuring because it requires us to believe that God is the author of our destiny, and his cosmic strategy and our personal fulfillment are miraculously interdependent; unsettling because it requires us to come up with a new prayer. If "God, use me!" is somewhat meaningless, it's at least earnest. Without this prayer and this framework of expectation to guide our decisions—"Once God hears that I *really* mean it, he'll launch me into my calling"—what are we to do? Where do we hang our hopes of one day walking into the calling God whispered in our ears so many years ago? Where do we direct our zeal for yielding our lives to his grand purpose? These are the questions I seek to answer in this book.

As associate pastor of New Life Church in Colorado Springs, I have the privilege of leading our Saturday-night service. At the top of the demographic bell curve on Saturday nights are people in their twenties and early thirties. (I am thirty-one.) Every Saturday I speak to several hundred wonderful, godly people about God's plan for the world and how their lives fit into it. And nearly every other day of the week, I sit across a table at Starbucks from one person and then another and another, and I listen to them explain how I was talking to them *personally* last week. "Pastor Rob, as you spoke, my heart was burning. I know God has called me to ________, but I'm stuck in this job doing ________, and I just don't know how to get from here to there. Maybe it was all a dream. Maybe this is all I'll ever do."

I get the feeling that these folks expected that after God called them, he would beam them out of their current lives and into the grandeur of their calling. Once some time passes and they haven't gotten beamed up, they get discouraged and either tuck their dream away in the hope chest and go on with life as usual, or they turn away from the dream completely and leave it to shrivel and die. Talking with so many people of my own age bracket over the past several years, I have become convinced that this confusion about our calling is endemic to the next generation of the body of Christ.

In truth, I am also a product of my generation. Thankfully, we are not the generation we have been painted to be. I am convinced from talking to my peers day after day in Starbucks after Starbucks that we are not the brainless Kurt Cobain–looking slackers that MTV has tried to convince the public we are. We are people who are dreaming big, trying hard, and looking for the way ahead.

There are two reasons why it encourages me to hear people of my generation ask me what to do to live into their dreams. First, it confirms that they're not slugs. Granted, there is no shortage of oxygen thieves out there, but I have seen and heard enough in my young pastoral career to know that not all people my age are plopped down in front of a PlayStation. The second reason is that, amazingly, I have something to tell them. One of the joys of pastoring is walking through difficult times with the people of God. Encouraging the sheep to lean on Jesus and assuring them of his sufficiency is the chief job of a shepherd. Yet these conversations are often bereft of specific, practical guidance. Conversations about cultivating our calling are not like that. Calling is a subject on which the Scriptures are replete with sometimes subtle, always applicable insights, and that makes it a delightful subject to talk about over a vanilla latte.

The reality is that one day—and perhaps sooner than you think—our generation will take the baton and start running. And the way we run the race will determine how well the church fulfills its calling. This is the reality that's shaping my purpose in life. I am vested in the belief that mine is "a chosen generation, a royal priesthood, a holy nation."[1] I think it serves God's people of every generation well to believe that this promise speaks to their day in the sun.

My hope in writing this book is twofold. First, that my elders who are running the race strong and sure will take heart and know that those in my generation are training hard in preparation for our lap around the track. We will be ready to take the baton when it's time, and we will not falter. Your work will not have been in vain.

Second, I hope that my own generation will realize that there *are* answers and there *is* direction to get us from here to there. You are not playing a giant roulette game, and you aren't in the hands of some capricious god who may or may not fulfill his promise depending on which way you turn at some unmarked intersection. God—who first tapped you on the shoulder and whispered in your ear—is faithful, and he will fulfill the dreams he gave you if you follow his guidelines. Your calling can be sure, and for the sake of a world that's living in darkness, it must be.

Ours is a pivotal generation—our watch comes at a crucial hour in the church's history—and we must be diligent and focused and do this thing right. We must run the race set before us, whatever that looks like for each of us individually. This means you cannot grow weary in laying hold of the dream of God that is churning in your heart. I know you still have a thousand questions. I can't give you the *what* or the *when,* but by God's grace, in this book I intend to give you the *how*—and that is the precursor to all the other answers. The insights I offer may not be very profound, but I offer them with the knowledge that they are scripturally mandated and they have worked in my own life. I trust by God's grace they will work in your life as well.

Chapter 2

Where Do I Go from Here?

> You are so young, so before all beginning, and I want to beg you...as much as I can, to be patient toward all that is unsolved in your heart and try to love the questions themselves like locked rooms and like books that are written in a very foreign tongue. Do not now seek the answers, which cannot be given to you because you would not be able to live them. And the point is, to live everything. Live the questions now. Perhaps you will then gradually, without noticing it, live along some distant day into the answer.
>
> —Rainer Maria Rilke, from *Letters to a Young Poet*

It started out like a typical day, but it ended unlike any other. David half listened at the breakfast table as his father and a couple of his older brothers discussed current events. Recent political developments had left the nation quite differently disposed, Israel's neighbors were uneasy, and the country's first king was mustering a national army. But none of this mattered much to David. His life was simple—sometimes wonderfully and sometimes agonizingly simple.

As Jesse's sons headed out to the fields, his brothers were abuzz with talk of war with the Philistines: One feared being drafted for combat; another was overflowing with excitement at the prospect of fighting for his people. The youngest of all the brothers, David had the sheep to worry about, and little else. He was responsible, hardy, and brave, and his father had entrusted the flock to his care some time ago. David waved to his big brothers as he parted ways with them, and then he headed toward the meadow where the sheep were grazing in the morning sun.

Long, lazy days under the Middle Eastern sun filled the gaps between exciting happenings. Relief from the monotony came when a sheep wandered off and David set out to find it, or when the occasional marauding lion or bear carried off some hapless victim from the flock, and David hunted down the invader. These were the fun days, but they weren't frequent. David spent most of his time writing and singing and dreaming about the world beyond the pasture.

And he would think about God. *What does he look like? What does he think about? How did he get all the water to go away after he flooded the earth with rain?* The stories David had heard about Noah and Abraham and Moses and Gideon captivated his imagination. *Such faith, such honor, such destiny—these men who were friends of God. Will people ever know God that way again? But times are different now. What ordinary man can get God's attention anymore?*

Out of the Blue

I wonder if David's thoughts ever drifted to his own destiny. He was young and obscure, but during the countless hours in the fields with the sheep—pleasant, safe, and ordinary moments—he dreamed the dreams of youth. *Will I be a shepherd forever? What if we really do wage war against the Philistines? I could help with that. I know how to fight, and I'm not afraid. Will I ever see faraway lands, meet with important people, marry a beautiful woman, or have a son of my own? O God of my fathers, what does my future hold?*

"David! *David!!!* "

Alarmed by the shrill call of one of his father's hired hands, David emerged from his daydream and snapped to attention.

"Your father needs you now!" the servant called out, panting for breath. "Hurry! Everyone's waiting for you!"

What on earth? What did I do now?! It's the guys—I know it. They set me up. I've been framed!

"Yes, what is it?"

Whatever it is, I didn't do it!

"The prophet...is here," replied the servant, still panting. "He...is asking for you!"

"What prophet?"

"The man of God...he is calling for you! He says that no one will sit down until you come! You must hurr—"

" *What* man of God?!"

Chapters 15 and 16 of 1 Samuel tell the story. God had responded to the Israelites' insistent request for a king, Saul had been anointed as Israel's leader, and shortly thereafter, God rejected Saul because of Saul's disobedience. In the wake of this upheaval, God spoke to his messenger, the prophet Samuel: "How long will you mourn for Saul, since I have rejected him as king over Israel? Fill your horn with oil and be on your way; I am sending you to Jesse of Bethlehem. I have chosen one of his sons to be king."[1]

All of this drama was unfolding while David was watching the sheep, oblivious. To say that he wasn't expecting the visit from Samuel is like saying you're not expecting a good-sized fish to come flying across the room and smack you in the head right now. It's hard to capture how out-of-the-blue it all must have been. Saul was offering up the burnt offering without waiting for Samuel, sparing King Agag in direct defiance of God's instructions, and generally making a mess of the kingship. David was playing music in a field somewhere. Like Luke Skywalker gazing up beyond the two suns of the planet Tatooine, his mind wandering from the droids he had recently acquired for his Uncle Owen to questions about the vast, exhilarating universe, David might have been dreaming of some more significant destiny. But he couldn't have known what was coming.

I love this part of David's life because it is the story of the unlikeliest moment imaginable. His interest piqued by the servant's words, David sped home from the pasture. From a distance he saw the scene just as the servant described it. His family was standing nervously in a circle, silent and wrapped in uneasiness. Next to his father leaned an old, austere man whom David presumed from the messenger's report to be Samuel. Samuel the legend, the last judge, the man who spoke to God. Samuel, the father of all Israel. *What is he doing here?*

The events that preceded being called in from the fields David could never have imagined. Samuel's narrative tells the story:

> When [Jesse and his sons] arrived, Samuel saw Eliab and thought, "Surely the LORD's anointed stands here before the LORD."
>
> But the LORD said to Samuel, "Do not consider his appearance or his height, for I have rejected him. The LORD does not look at the things man looks at. Man looks at the outward appearance, but the LORD looks at the heart."
>
> Then Jesse called Abinadab and had him pass in front of Samuel. But Samuel said, "The LORD has not chosen this one either." Jesse then had Shammah pass by, but Samuel said, "Nor has the LORD chosen this one." Jesse had seven of his sons pass before Samuel, but Samuel said to him, "The LORD has not chosen these." So he asked Jesse, "Are these all the sons you have?"
>
> "There is still the youngest," Jesse answered, "but he is tending the sheep."
>
> Samuel said, "Send for him; we will not sit down until he arrives."
>
> So he sent and had him brought in.[2]

As David approached the place where the others were gathered, his curiosity got the best of him and he broke into a run. When the prophet saw him, the stoic countenance of the old man yielded to an intensity that both alarmed and invigorated David. He arrived at the gathering out of breath and eager to learn what everyone else seemed to know. He noticed the disdain on his brothers' faces, wondered what that was all about, locked eyes with the old prophet, and saw a coy expression that surprised and delighted him. As if to suggest he knew something infinitely important that the rest of the world ought to want to know, the leathery seer pierced Jesse's youngest son with an impossibly certain glare and—*Am I reading this guy right?*—the slightest hint of a smile.

Perhaps it was the young man's appearance—"ruddy, with a fine appearance and handsome features"—that captured the old man's attention, or maybe some other quality the world will never know. Whatever happened at that moment inside the prophet Samuel, David couldn't have been more confounded by what unfolded:

> The LORD said, "Rise and anoint him; he is the one."
>
> So Samuel took the horn of oil and anointed him in the presence of his brothers, and from that day on the Spirit of the LORD came upon David in power. Samuel then went to Ramah.[3]

Who would have imagined such a thing that morning at breakfast? David awoke that day a boy, full of naive, boyish dreams, and he went to bed a king. God chose David, set him apart for this time and this purpose, and when the time came, he grabbed the young shepherd's attention. God tapped David on the shoulder and said, in effect, "You're not going to do what you thought you were going to do. You're going to serve me for the rest of your life. And you're going to love it."

Now What?

What's all the more amazing to me in this drama is that immediately after applying the oil to the unsuspecting adolescent, Samuel just...left. Went to Ramah. Imagine the scene after Samuel departed. What do you do now? What do you talk about at the dinner table? David got called in from the fields, learned that he was God's choice to be Israel's next king, and had oil poured over his head. He got the surprise of a lifetime, and then—*poof!*—the prophet disappeared. As mysteriously and abruptly as the bizarre encounter began, it was over, and David was left to figure out what to do next.

During the 1980s, there was a fabulous, short-lived television program called *The Greatest American Hero.* The premise was that an alien spacecraft landed briefly on Earth, delivered to an average-Joe American guy a red suit that imbued him with super powers, and then left. The twist was that the alien benefactors didn't give the guy any instructions for how to use the suit. They just swooped in, dropped off the suit, and flew away, leaving the protagonist to figure it all out by himself. The show's theme song gave voice to the hero's inner plight as he considered in disbelief what had happened to him (it's embarrassing that I remember this!):

> Suddenly I'm up on top of the world,
> Should have been somebody else.[4]

David must have felt like that. In one day, in one minute, his entire world changed forever. That night sleep must have come slowly. How do you begin processing something so unexpected, so unprecedented? *I suppose I'll live like royalty now. Will I have servants? Will I have to go to war? And how does one learn to be king, anyway? Is there some prep school I can go to? Will I be rich? Will God speak to me?* On and on the questions would surely go, excitement growing with each one. David was a man hardwired for destiny, and now for the first time, he had a kingly destiny to pursue.

Samuel's dramatic and unexpected visit to Jesse's household when he singled out David and anointed him as king was clearly an act of God. So why shouldn't David have expected the next step to be just as dramatic and miraculous? Being identified as God's choice to lead his people had a galvanizing effect on David's faith. After that, it was no trouble imagining that God would do something equally unlikely the next day to make the transition happen. In fact, it was hard to imagine anything else.

As David lay on his bed that night, he probably assumed that the next day he would get a visit from members of the king's court who would load him into a gold-crested chariot and take him to the royal palace.[5] Once you've seen the fairy godmother, you kind of expect the pumpkin to get turned into a carriage.

But if the previous day's events had been completely unexpected, a bigger surprise came in the morning when David strode confidently out of his house, looked around for the prophet or the army or the heavenly host itself, and found...nothing. No angels had swooped down from heaven to whisk David away into his new position. No royal escort had arrived to take him back to the palace. The man of God hadn't even made a follow-up visit to explain what David should expect to happen next. Nothing.

If David's world turned upside down yesterday, today it turned right side up again with no explanation whatever. Equally excited and befuddled, David now faced the decision of whether to return to his life as a shepherd and pretend that yesterday never happened or to play out the drama and see where it would lead. But honestly, how do you go back? The words of the prophet resonated in David's heart like a note he had never fully recognized until this moment. For the first time in his life, he was awake to the purpose he had sought since his youth. The vague but pervasive sense of destiny that had haunted his dreams finally crystallized and shook him, and the feeling was exhilarating. No, he couldn't go back now, because nothing was left for him there. He had awakened to a larger world that was more real than anything he had ever experienced, and he couldn't pretend that nothing had happened any more than Frodo could go back to the Shire after learning about the ring of power. David had found his destiny, and now he had only one option: to wait and see what would happen next.

Three Paradigms for Waiting

David faced a situation so many of us find ourselves in. We've heard from God—he came and tapped us on the shoulder one day out of the clear blue and revealed something to us that, to some extent, clarified our destiny. Now we are left to figure out how to live into that calling. Many of us assumed that the next step would miraculously unfold before us. When it didn't, we had to figure out what to do next.

What do you do with a dream you've received from God? You wait. In the next two chapters, I will share three paradigms I see people adopt, consciously or unconsciously, as they wait on the fulfillment of the dreams of God: (1) manhandle the plans, (2) wait fifteen minutes and forget the plans, and (3) super-spiritualize the plans.

Chapter 3

Manhandling the Plans

Oh, the waiting is the hardest part.

—'80s rocker Tom Petty

You know how it works. God whispers into your heart and gently fades away. Then you take off running with the calling as if you're afraid the whole thing will go away if you stop, and invariably you end up leaving God in the dust.[1]

Remember when we were young and we played church-league basketball? (By the way, did you ever see a more brutal and acrimonious bunch than the people who played church league? I mean to tell you, the surest way I know to see blood let is to get a bunch of Christians together to compete in recreational sports!) Okay, remember the guy who would get the ball, put his head down, start dribbling frenetically around the court, and never look up to see what was going on? That's the person who tries to manhandle God's plans. He hears something from God—a whisper, an inclination, a vapor of direction—and he is off to the races. Just the notion that God might once have thought about using him in a certain way is enough for this forger of well-laid plans. In fact, if he were honest he'd tell you that he actually had it all mapped out beforehand; his car was tuned and his engine revving, and he was just waiting for the green flag from heaven.

To the manhandler, waiting on the Lord is a weak excuse for lethargy and inaction. "God can't steer a parked car" is his mantra, and under this banner he informs the Creator of the universe of his intent, graciously offers God the briefest opportunity to adjust anything he might need to, and then charges ahead. This guy tells himself—and usually countless others—that he is walking by faith, and he can very often be found enumerating his exploits for the kingdom.

In the Scriptures, the classic manhandler of God's plans was Saul. Soon after becoming Israel's first king, he led the people into battle against their nemesis, the Philistines:

> The Philistines assembled to fight Israel, with three thousand chariots, six thousand charioteers, and soldiers as numerous as the sand on the seashore. They went up and camped at Micmash, east of Beth Aven. When the men of Israel saw that their situation was critical and that their army was hard pressed, they hid in caves and thickets, among the rocks, and in pits and cisterns. Some Hebrews even crossed the Jordan to the land of Gad and Gilead.
>
> Saul remained at Gilgal, and all the troops with him were quaking with fear. He waited seven days, the time set by Samuel; but Samuel did not come to Gilgal, and Saul's men began to scatter. So he said, "Bring me the burnt offering and the fellowship offerings." And Saul offered up the burnt offering.[2]

Eager to bring victory to Israel and firmly establish his leadership, the chronically overzealous king took the prophet's duty into his own hands and ended up botching the whole thing:

> Just as he finished making the offering, Samuel arrived, and Saul went out to greet him.
>
> "What have you done?" asked Samuel.
>
> Saul replied, "When I saw that the men were scattering, and that you did not come at the set time, and that the Philistines were assembling at Micmash, I thought, 'Now the Philistines will come down against me at Gilgal, and I have not sought the LORD's favor.' So I felt compelled to offer the burnt offering."
>
> "You acted foolishly," Samuel said. "You have not kept the command the LORD your God gave you; if you had, he would have established your kingdom over Israel for all time. But now

> your kingdom will not endure; the LORD has sought out a man
> after his own heart and appointed him leader of his people,
> because you have not kept the LORD's command."[3]

As was his tendency, Saul manhandled the plans—took upon himself the direction and the work of God—and this habit eventually cost him the kingdom.

It is interesting that when God finally wearied of Saul and stripped him of the throne, these are the words he spoke through Samuel to the blunt and bumbling leader:

> Does the LORD delight in burnt offerings and sacrifices
> as much as in obeying the voice of the LORD?
> To obey is better than sacrifice,
> and to heed is better than the fat of rams....
> Because you have rejected the word of the LORD,
> he has rejected you as king.[4]

Therein lies the problem with manhandling the plans. At its core it is disobedience or, at best, coincidental obedience. The one who manhandles the plans tells God, in effect, "Thanks for the advice. I'll take it from here." And too often this is the result: You get to a place in your life where the engine is stalled and you can't get it started again and you look back to see where you went wrong. Then, in a moment of lucidity and self-awareness, you realize that you left God at a crossroads ten years back. But God's response to sustained, unrepentant disobedience is rejection. He is not in the business of foisting himself on us and compelling us to obey; he whispers his guidance and gives us the choice to follow him, to seek our own path, or to consider his direction and manhandle the plans. The stories of people who have been rejected by God because they took the plans and manhandled them are particularly sad. Unlike someone who squanders his or her life on abject disobedience, the manhandler responds to the genuine call from God and starts down the incomparably fulfilling road of living into that calling, but then charges ahead and leaves the Caller in the dust.

At this point I have to confess that I know a thing or two more than the next guy about manhandling the plans. I have debated as to whether I would include a personal story to illustrate my point. But since it is the consummate "I, too, have manhandled the plans" story, and one of the two or three defining events of my life so far, it would be almost dishonest not to share it. So to that prickly subject and all the catharsis its writing promises me I now turn.

The Unbelievable Faux-Wedding Story

Everybody has at least one unbelievable story. This is mine. My wife… um…called off our wedding on the wedding day. There. I said it. I gave you the bottom line up front. Now if this is uninteresting to you, it won't offend me at all if you skip ahead to the next chapter for the second paradigm.

Okay, here we go. Now, by virtue of the fact that I referred to her as "my wife," you know that Mauri and I did end up getting married. But to get the full impact of this story, you have to understand the mind-set of a single man of twenty-five years who had generally made good decisions in life (translation: I was a virgin) and was duly eager to wed. I had found the woman I loved, exhausted every means at my disposal to persuade her to love me, and finally won her heart. The blessing and curse was that *I knew* she was to be my wife. I knew that I knew that I knew.

I knew because, in truth, God had shown me in a dramatic, unmistakable, unforgettable way.

It was the summer of 1997 and I was an officer in the United States Army. After I graduated from college, the army sent me to Colorado Springs to lead a tank platoon at Fort Carson. (I paid for college with an Army ROTC scholarship. So I should say, *you* paid for my college. Thank you! Then I paid you back by blowing things up with tanks and defending your freedom for the ensuing four years.)

During those days, I spent weeks at a time in remote, desolate places around the country with a group of strong, honorable men, waging fake wars to hone our skills. Well, during one of those field-training exercises, God spoke to me in an unexpected way. It was, in fact, the first time since the Princess-Leia-esque visitation on the plains of East Africa, and the experience was equally mind-blowing. There I was standing in the turret of my M1A1 Abrams Tank, clad in a flame-retardant battle suit, with night-vision goggles affixed to my combat-vehicle-crewman's helmet, terrain map and red-lens, low-detection flashlight in hand, awaiting orders to cross the line of departure. It was 3:45 a.m.

God seems to select the moments when I would least expect an epiphany from heaven to speak to me. Sure, it's true. In those days there was no shortage of moments during which I was indeed thinking about women, but words can't describe how thoroughly *not* one of those moments this was. I was thinking about the battle that was about to happen. I was thinking about sleep. I might even have been thinking about how I hadn't showered in eleven days. But I was so completely *not* thinking about marriage that I was entirely befuddled when the topic suddenly came to mind. Then it occurred to me: *It's happening again.* And for the next few seconds, the same sense of categorical certainty that marked the Africa incident descended on me again. In that brief window of spiritual lucidity, it became clear—in a way I cannot sufficiently explain—that my new acquaintance Mauri Hallman was to become my wife. Looking back, I see that this experience was astonishingly distinct from any direction God had ever given me before or has given me since. So far from the usual whisper or slight nudge (you know, the sort that leaves you questioning whether that was really God), this encounter had the effect of a one-hundred-foot flashing neon sign being placed right in front of me. The sign said just this: Marry Mauri. And then—*poof!*—just like before, it was gone.

I was so staggered by what had happened and so concerned that I wouldn't believe it later on (it might have been heatstroke or eating too many meals with a shelf life of thirty-seven years), I pulled out my waterproof camouflage field notebook and hastily scrawled down the experience in a letter to Mauri. Here's what it said:

9 July 97

Mauri,

I write this now with the strictest intent to keep it from you until…such a time as it would be right for you to read it. I am at Fort Irwin for the month of July. We just spoke last night. Our friendship/relationship is at a point of decision. You have received a "hold" from God. I am trying to figure out what to do. This is the setting.

The startling thing is that I see now that you will be my wife. You should know that this is not a common type of revelation for me. But—and how I'm not sure—today it has just…settled upon me, occurred to me that this is what is to happen. And because if you are reading this, that means we are married and I can tell you I am looking forward to marrying you in a huge way. So when I have said that this situation scares me a little, this is what I am referring to. I am so eager to get to know you, to see how it will all unfold, and to love you the way God intended for you to be loved. Mauri, you are a treasure, and I can't really imagine feeling like I deserve you. I thank God for you, and I pledge now to try hard to be patient and wait for you and the Lord (you're probably laughing, because I probably wasn't patient at all). I have a feeling that, by God's grace, you and I are going to do some big work for the kingdom together.

Until...whenever—and always,

Rob

As I was finishing the letter, the orders to begin movement came crackling over the radio. I ripped the pages out of my notebook, tucked them away in the breast pocket of my battle suit, put the whole episode out of my mind, and ordered my driver to move out.

A couple of weeks later, home from the field exercise, I was about to throw my battle suit into the washing machine when I remembered that enigmatic, hastily scrawled missive tucked in the breast pocket and that enigmatic dawn in the desert of Southern California when I wrote it. I pulled out the tattered and dirty page, shook my head in bewilderment, and put it in an envelope. I proceeded to seal it, write on the front of the envelope "DO NOT OPEN UNTIL OUR WEDDING DAY," and put it in the bottom of my sock drawer for safekeeping.

What transpired that morning in the California desert would have been amazing even if Mauri and I had been in a committed relationship; it was all the more amazing considering that we barely knew each other. Don't get me wrong—I was crazy about her from the first day we met.

But we weren't at the "What would you think about getting married?" stage yet. We hadn't even shared a dessert. So I was faced with the problem of *What do I do now?*

It's important to note here that I held a deep-rooted loathing for using "God told me" to try to win a woman's affection. Being a veteran of a college campus Christian fellowship group (those of you who were in college campus Christian fellowship groups know exactly what I mean), I had witnessed this happen many times, always with unfortunate results. In the wake of so many spiritual daters, I had made a solemn vow before the Lord of hosts that I would never use "God told me," or any variation or permutation thereof, to influence a woman's decision about loving me. May God strike me down, may dogs eat my flesh, and may I be buried in a shallow unmarked grave if anything but genuine affection moved a girl to like me.

This, of course, created the problem of getting Mauri to like me. God had given me the plans. The calling was there to be lived into, and I just had to live it. So I set about the ironic business of winning Mauri without using "God told me" when God had, in fact, told me. What followed was a massive, unparalleled manhandling of the plans.

In the season that followed my revelation on the tank, I wooed Mauri. I skied deftly in front of her on group ski days. I shimmied across the very high, very steep roof of the five-story Victorian-house-turned-apartment-complex in which she resided and dropped down onto the not-really-meant-to-be-used balcony outside her window and read poetry to her. I tried to be as impressive as possible. For the next two years, I tirelessly laid siege to the bulwark of that woman's affections.

But as I've mentioned, Mauri wasn't too into me at first. In fact, there came a time when I decided it was do or die, and with all the melodrama of a made-for-TV movie, I looked her dead in the eye, hushed my voice to achieve the perfect wispiness for the moment, and recited these lines to her:

> Mauri, I know that deep down inside you have feelings for me that you are suppressing. We've been dancing around them now for several months, and I'm done. It's time to face the music. So Mauri, if you can look me in the eye and tell me that it's not happening now, it's not happening ever, and you feel nothing for me, I'll go away and leave you alone forever. But if you can't—and I believe there's no way you can say that—then let's love each other.

So she looked me in the eye, and with maddening matter-of-factness she repeated my words back to me: "It's not happening now, it's not happening ever, and—what was the last part? Oh yeah, I feel nothing for you." Just like that. She didn't even pause to think about it! *How can this be? What about my Princess Leia encounter on the tank that summer? This is not going well at all...* So I went home that night, thought about it a little, and concluded that this could only mean one thing: It's time for a change of tactics.

For the next year I tried every approach, every angle—"You know you need me," "Let's build the kingdom of God together," "Would you consider faking it?"—and every persona—boyish diffidence, aloof confidence, puppy-dog attentiveness. And one day, one magical day, the most amazing thing happened. She said, "You're right. I have had deeply suppressed feelings for you all along." *Wow! How about that? I was right! The Princess-Leia-apparition-like experience is money!* So we decided to pursue a relationship and see what would happen.

The arduous wooing process afforded us ample opportunity to get to know each other, so I saw no reason for delay. I had worked hard for two years to conquer Fort Mauri, and now there seemed no sense in delaying the occupation. So when the drama of pursuit at last culminated in a relationship, I did what any self-respecting suitor two years on his knee beneath the balcony would do: I waited the obligatory three weeks and then asked her to marry me. Who had time for dating, and what was the purpose? I *knew,* and now, it seemed, she did too.

The proposal and the three weeks after she had said yes were undramatic—but not so the rest of the engagement. Mauri said yes to me because she felt obligated to. She had said no for so long, and now that she did indeed love me, she wanted badly to say yes to something. But she knew. She knew I was manhandling the plans, and she knew the potential fallout.

After the proposal dust settled and we began to see things as they were, problems arose almost immediately:

1. The whole basis of our relationship over the past two years had been adversarial.
2. Mauri's parents imagined her marrying someone...um... different—as in, other than me.
3. Mauri wanted to do ministry, and I wore camouflage to work every day.
4. I had a very unusual roommate who secretly loved Mauri but wouldn't acknowledge it, and when she chose me, he waged a sort of spiritual sabotage by prophesying to everyone but the pope that we were out of God's will.
5. Both of our families were reticent about our marrying because they didn't know one another or their child's choice of spouse.

All of these issues defined our engagement, but they didn't have to. Every one of them would have worked itself out just fine—in the proper time. Our families are godly and honorable and would have backed us unwaveringly—if they had had the chance to spend some time with us first. My calling away from the army and into the ministry would have become evident—if we had let it unfold. Even my unusual roommate would have come to terms with his surreptitious designs on Mauri's affections—if there had been time. Instead, all of these hotspots erupted together at the surprising news of our engagement. So at a time when most couples go to wedding shows, have parties thrown for them, and spend afternoons gazing longingly into each other's eyes, we did battle. We sparred with each other, with our families, with our friends, with everybody. Manhandling the plans turned our engagement into a war.

The plot thickened when, as you would expect, the stress of everyone's opinions caught up with Mauri. The us-against-the-world levee inevitably gave way, and the floodwaters of doubt, fear, and uncertainty came crashing into the happy hamlet of our loving relationship. It was at this juncture during our engagement that Mauri made a decision that escalated our troubles. And here the story takes a turn for the bizarre. Understandably fraught with concern and beginning to wonder if she had made a horrible mistake, Mauri called up an old friend of the family who is, apparently, a self-appointed Old Testament–style oracle of God—a personal prophet, not much different in effect from Dionne Warwick and the Psychic Hotline. (I am at this point exercising every faculty of will not to veer into sharp criticism of this type of silliness. So I won't say how this man's abuse of a scriptural office undoes the Reformation and, for that matter, the New Testament. And I won't go into the lunacy of inviting people to bring their marriage-partner candidates to you and telling them on behalf of God whether they've chosen the right person.)

Well, as you can imagine, The Prophet didn't make things any smoother for Mauri and me. He was no dummy, though. He was crafty and subtle. Presumably, he knew that if he were to say, "Don't marry him;

he's a loser," his words wouldn't hold water. Whatever legitimate accusations could be made against me, it could be firmly proven that I was not an ax murderer, a drug abuser, someone who kicks house pets, or any other form of indigent. No, The Prophet instead offered this problematic prognostication to my beleaguered wife-to-be: "He is a good man, and you would have a good life together. But he is not *God's best.*" The Prophet's words sprayed gasoline on the sparking tinder of Mauri's doubts and fears, and it wasn't long before the ensuing wildfire spread throughout her whole family and raged completely out of control.

So, to recap, we had

- two hesitant families (one family whose uncertainty about me had been newly fueled by The Prophet, and the other who was growing more concerned because of the growing concern of the first family),
- two false prophets (the unusual now-ex-roommate, and the man known to me by the ominous moniker "The Prophet"),
- a horde of friends forming opinions about our chances of making it (due mainly to the "ministry" of false prophet number 1, also known as the unusual ex-roommate),
- a flotilla of relatives and family friends forming opinions about our chances of making it (these were, in truth, chiefly on the *no* end of the opinion spectrum, due mainly to the "ministry" of false prophet number 2, also known as The Prophet), and, of course,
- Mauri, her heart increasingly stirred with the noble theme of overseas missions, and me, my heart stirred by the destruction of a Soviet-era T-72 combat vehicle at a range of three kilometers.

We were a mess.

This disaster rambled on and continued to escalate for the duration of our engagement. It is important to note that in my mission focus I may have failed to notice the red flags here and there. Several times during those tumultuous months, for instance, Mauri sent up subtle signals faintly recognizable on the distant horizon—signals such as breaking down into convulsive sobs while managing to get out the words, "We have got to stop this madness!" and occasionally targeting me with projectiles while articulating my bullish imperviousness to any common sense. I now recognize these signals as opportunities to stop manhandling the plans, submit to God's leading, and get the thing back on track, but at the time I missed them and manhandled on.

Such was the state of our affairs up to the week of the wedding. Now try to imagine the scene. People flew in from all over the country. Bridesmaids and groomsmen bought dresses and rented tuxedos. Showers, bachelor parties, dinners with the families—all of the normal wedding-week activities transpired, but everyone knew that this situation was far from normal. The flurry of the week's activities barely masked the tension underlying the entire affair, but everybody tried to pretend and make things go as smoothly as possible. The rehearsal dinner was a scene from a Ben Stiller movie. And then everyone went to bed, secretly looking forward to the relief they'd feel when the whole affair was over.

The day of the wedding arrived. That morning, nine groomsmen and I headed to the YMCA to play basketball, nine bridesmaids gathered in a house to do to themselves whatever women do to themselves for seven hours before a wedding, the out-of-town guests drove the Pikes Peak Highway and bought overpriced trinkets in Old Colorado City, the cake lady delivered the cake to the reception hall, the caterer set up the buffet, the band members arranged their instruments and equipment near the dance floor, the decorators decorated, and Mauri sat with her mother and wept.

What came next hit me like the kind of ocean breaker that crested before you could brace yourself when you were a kid, that knocked you right off your feet and sent you tumbling in the salty water, your eyes burning, water up your nose, and totally disoriented until—*thunk!*—your head thumped the hard, sandy bottom, and you surfaced, stunned, only to realize later how much you hurt all over.

I had returned from the gym with the guys, gotten cleaned up, and was heading out the door for the before-the-wedding photos, the black vinyl tuxedo bag draped over my shoulder and hanging from my index finger, when the phone rang.

"I can't do it..."

What happened? What could possibly have happened this morning that was bad enough to cause this? There's no way this can actually be happening...

My heart tumbled around inside me for a while.

Soon came the gradual, awful realization that a totally different question mattered: *How could I not have seen it?* All the warning signs were there. We hadn't even been happy for a couple of months. I had just kept driving, which is what manhandlers do. They drive and drive and don't consider any of the benefits of waiting productively for the unfolding of God's plan.

But I ought to finish the story: I found myself numb and incredulous. *Surely not. This is insane. This doesn't happen to real people. This happens in unimaginative romantic comedies that fly off the shelf at Blockbuster. Forget it. There's no way. All the people...all the food...all the preparations...us. I'm not going down without a fight.*

So I drove over to my flummoxed fiancée's house—or rather I watched myself drive there from the silenced omniscient narrator's point of view that became my soul's perch—to say something like, "Surely you must be joking," and hope that seeing me and having to say the awful thing to my face would somehow snap her out of her trance. When I arrived, I saw myself get the crushing fullness of the message when her mother intercepted my approach to the house and graciously informed me that it would be best if Mauri and I not see each other. I remember briefly thinking about sneaking in a back window and then realizing with deadening finality that the wedding really was not going to happen.

It was at this juncture that I descended into one of the few bouts of genuine depression in my life. This is weird, but the omniscient me took a quirky pleasure in the novelty of real depression, so I sought out the most depressing habitat in which to experience my dejection, and that turned out to be Denny's. Kids were laughing and eating big pancakes in the nonsmoking section (where I would ordinarily sit were I compelled at gunpoint to dine at Denny's), and that didn't seem depressing enough, so I asked for smoking. My eyes stung. I ordered black coffee. What could be more depressing? The coffee was bitter and my eyes burned from the smoke, and I sat there thinking for a long, long time. This is where in the unimaginative Tom Hanks movie, a tear would roll down my cheek as I thought about all that I had lost—but that didn't happen. I knew I hadn't lost anything, that we still loved each other and that we would get married someday. I knew the days that followed Denny's would be embarrassing and emotional and annoying. And worst of all, I knew that this was my doing.

As you already know, we did end up getting married. After about three weeks apart, we met at a coffee shop, cried, apologized, and began piecing our relationship back together. We went through a second round of premarital counseling, figuring that we obviously needed it, and then we started replanning the wedding. One of the trickier parts of doing this a second time was persuading skeptical sisters, dubious dads, and bewildered bridesmaids that we really were right for each other. We re-invited the guests, re-booked the honeymoon, re-chose the catering, reordered the tuxes. Then, at last, eight months after the first attempt, we got married. It was a wonderful day.

You could say that this is a case of "all's well that ends well," but that would diminish the lessons of our tumultuous premarital saga. We were married in the end, it is true, and we have never questioned the rightness of that decision. But I made it much harder than it needed to be, and that left lasting scars.

Yes, friends, I have manhandled the plans, and how it cost me. The complicated, hurtful, and embarrassing season that followed the faux-wedding (as it is now called in New Life Church lore) did pass, and we did get married, and we are now quite happy. But, oh, what needless misery and, worse, what wasted time! It is tempting to receive the plans from God and manhandle them, but doing so practically guarantees that you will be the recipient of that particular kind of character sharpening that happens most often in the wake of phenomenal heartbreak or public humiliation or, worst of all, both.

Chapter 4

More Ways You Don't Want to Wait on the Lord

> If you are not too long, I will wait here for you all my life.
>
> —Oscar Wilde

Now that I've purged my soul and given you a good example of manhandling the plans from personal experience, let's move on to the other two paradigms for waiting on the Lord.

Wait Fifteen Minutes and Forget the Plans

The second paradigm for waiting parallels the story Jesus told about the seed that fell on the rocky places where the soil was shallow. The plants quickly sprang up, but they soon withered.[1] Likewise, these recipients of a dream from God respond to his whispering with a flare of passion and dedication to wait on him, but their response is largely show. When nothing happens for a few days, the plans promptly take the back burner, and then they are entirely forgotten when something more exciting presents itself. If those who manhandle the plans are overinterested, these dreamers are underinterested.

In my view, waiting fifteen minutes and forgetting the plans is the most common mishandling of the dreams God entrusts to us. You see it all the time: God whispers in someone's ear, and at first the person is all fired up. He prays and fasts and seeks God and burns with holy passion, determined to carry out the plans he believes the Creator laid for him from before the foundations of the earth. Zealous for the plans, he waits impatiently and often looks around the corner. He talks quite a bit about the plans. Then when he wakes up one morning with the same realizations young David had—no flaming chariot is bound for his doorstep to transport him to the palace, everything is exactly the same as it was before he received the plans, and somehow he has to live into the calling of God he has received, perhaps even over the course of years—he cuts bait and walks away.

Interestingly, the forgetter of the plans is seldom conflicted or sad when he walks away. To respond that way, I suppose, would be to admit that *he* had in some way missed them. This is not the way of the forgetter. Neither, incidentally, does he run away with his tail between his legs. No, the one who waits fifteen minutes and forgets the plans is not going to take responsibility for missing them. He waited, and God didn't show up. Now he simply moves on—no harm, no foul—and doesn't speak of the plans anymore. He forgets because he chooses to.

I am a devoted fan of Larry Bird, the legendary forward for the Boston Celtics in the 1980s. I loved his career as a professional basketball player, and I love watching him now as a coach. Understand, I grew up in the Boston area in the 1980s, when the tension and hostility between the Celtics and the Los Angeles Lakers—of Magic Johnson, Kareem Abdul-Jabbar, and James Worthy vintage—were second only to the Cold War that had for some forty years held the United States and the Soviet Union deadlocked on the brink of global thermonuclear annihilation. This was the basketball rivalry of the ages because it represented something bigger than the two teams or even the East and West Coasts. It spoke of the future and the past, tradition and innovation. The sport I love so well was at a crossroads, and the animosity between these two teams and the cities they represented sat in the middle of the intersection. The Celtics were where basketball had come from, the Lakers were where it was going, and the two teams reviled each other. These were fabulous years to be a lover of the game.

Over the years I have learned much from the way Larry Bird approached the game and the way he played it. I think the essence of his greatness and imitability (for certainly, I had no hope of ever being six feet nine inches tall or of playing in the NBA) was captured in the title of his autobiography *Drive.* That quality is what made Larry Bird great.

There were bigger, stronger, and faster players on every team he played against, yet consistently over his career, he outproduced, outscored, outwon them all. He was dominant because he was the best pure shooter in the history of the game, and he shot the lights out game after game, year after year because of his tenacious, otherworldly drive. In his words:

> One thing I've never really understood since I began playing basketball is why more players don't make the effort to become reliable free throw shooters. It just takes practice and hard work. And concentration.
>
> Some guys seem to take missing free throws for granted. They'll say, "I'll take my chances when I get there." Or "I don't get fouled much, so why worry about it?" I can't understand that type of thinking.[2]

Larry Bird got the vision and never, never let go. It had been said that even in the twilight of his career, he would come to the Boston Garden two hours earlier than the other players just to practice his shot. I remember as a teenager wanting to see this for myself, so I dragged my father into the city one Saturday afternoon two hours earlier than we actually needed to arrive at the arena. We got the best spot in the parking garage, bought an overpriced bratwurst from a vendor on the street, bought an overpriced, large, foamy green extended index finger emblazoned with the Celtics logo, and made our way into the Garden and upstairs to floor level. I entered the arena with all the excitement of a teenage girl at a John Mayer concert. Finding the courtside area designated for the fans who were dedicated enough to arrive for Larry's pre-warmup ritual, my dad and I were rewarded with an unforgettable experience. For almost an hour, Bird staged a clinic on dedication and tenacity as he methodically went around and around and around the perimeter, firing one shot after another. He never missed. In close, behind the three-point mark, from the free-throw line, jump shot, set shot, turnaround, fadeaway, off the backboard, perfect swish. It was breathtaking to watch. Larry Bird achieved epic stature in my fifteen-year-old mind that day—a position he never surrendered. But something also happened in me that went beyond admiration. Burned into my psyche was a reverence for getting a vision, holding on tight, and never, never letting go.

At its core, forgetting the plans is the same sin as manhandling them. The manhandler disobeys God by his action; the forgetter disobeys by his inaction. In effect, both of these characters err by forgetting God. The manhandler overresponds to the plans out of his enthusiasm to get going, but he underresponds to—or forgets—God, leaving him in the dust. The forgetter rejects the plans and, implicitly, the one who gave them to him. For different reasons, both mismanagers of God's plans fall by the same sword: a fundamental lack of the fear of the Lord.

Super-Spiritualize the Plans

The third paradigm for waiting on the Lord is the most dangerous because it is the most insidious: super-spiritualizing the plans. The super-spiritualizer is familiar to you and me: He is the one who is ultra-in-tune with the Holy Spirit, is especially facile with spiritual language, and is uncommonly cognizant of the spiritual implications of everything. He can often be heard telling people wispily about the Big Things God is doing, and for a while you are in awe of that and even wish God would do such Big Things in your own life. But eventually you start to question why you never can pin down exactly what the Big Things are. Sometime after that you realize that the Big Things are always nebulous because they are nothing, and eventually you see that they are just an excuse not to engage, a sort of noble-appearing barrier between the super-spiritualizer and reality. An imaginary friend.

The super-spiritualizer receives the plans and prays about them. And prays about them some more. And talks about them. And talks about praying about them. And prays about talking about them. But the problem is that he never does them. He and the manhandler (whose watchword, remember, is "God can't steer a parked car") are at opposite poles. The guiding principle of the super-spiritualizer is to wait on the Lord. He is persuaded of the error of the manhandlers and views himself as more enlightened in the ways of God. He knows that Jesus did only what he saw the Father doing and said only what he heard the Father saying. Consequently, the super-spiritualizer waits for the Father to do or say something specific and obvious before he does or says anything. This philosophy sounds good—and it *is* good—but the super-spiritualizer misapplies it. He distorts the scriptural principle to justify his inactivity, and he constructs around himself a force field to guard against and assuage deep, controlling fear. Fear is at the root of the impotence I've seen in all super-spiritualizers—fear of missing God's will, fear of failing, fear of being viewed as unspiritual. So they keep for themselves a spiritual trump card, they wait on the Lord for a stone-tablet revelation or a visitation from the heavenly host, and all the while, they talk about the Big Things God is doing.

You need to understand that I'm not criticizing spirituality. I'm in the spirituality business, and I spend the bulk of my time encouraging people to pursue the things of God. The Bible itself clearly states that the things of the Spirit are spiritually discerned, and Jesus said that true worshipers must worship the Father in spirit and in truth.[3] What I seek to point out here is an error in understanding that infects and immobilizes the body of Christ, and that is pseudospirituality. This great derailer of callings and inhibitor of the genuine work of God is the true heartbeat of the super-spiritualizers, and it is doubly noxious because it is both corrosive for individual believers and contagious to the entire body. Pseudospiritual people are fond of symbols and code language, and they are usually attractive to new believers because they seem to be in close touch with the deep things of God. Very often they create a sort of aura that mesmerizes and inspires and draws people in, and they have substantial interpersonal influence. The hallmark of the more charismatic super-spiritualizers—by this I mean possessing charisma, not speaking in tongues and dancing in worship services—is an eager following of apprentice super-spiritualizers. Like so many others, this error in understanding is cancerous—both in its propensity to spread throughout the body and in its detrimental effect on people's lives.

My aforementioned unusual ex-roommate was a super-spiritualizer of the plans. On many occasions he would prostrate himself before the Lord in a grandiose style that was very inspiring. I met him when I was a young army officer and was hungry for the things of God. To my Presbyterian sensibilities, his passion for God's voice and his apparently fine-tuned ability to hear it were overwhelmingly appealing. I was drawn to him immediately. It didn't seem to matter that he was chronically cash strapped and perpetually popping in to stay with this or that friend for a season (everything was always "for a season"—this is very spiritual). All that mattered was that he was waiting to hear from God, and he was poised for this to happen at any moment. Presumably, once he heard from God, he would start down the road of the grand calling that was, it seemed, even too wonderful to talk about in any detail. For him it was unquestionably a matter of Big Things that God was doing—and it always was. My ex-roommate was wonderfully good-natured and pleasant to be around, and he possessed a mountain of talent that God doubtless desired to use for his glory. No doubt about it, he *was* called. It wasn't that he was a bad person or, God knows, an incapable one. It was rather, in the immortal words of F. Scott Fitzgerald who introduced America to the Great Jay Gatsby, "what preyed on [him], what foul dust floated in the wake of his dreams."[4] That "foul dust" was a perpetual state of inactivity and fear that left his God-given dreams—and most other productive endeavors—always over the next hill.

The three paradigms we've discussed—manhandling the plans, forgetting the plans, and super-spiritualizing the plans—are just some of the things not to do in the name of waiting on the Lord. They are deep, miry pits covered by a thin layer of brush on the trail toward God's calling for our lives. They will swallow you up and wear you down and waste precious years. They are perilous. I've watched them ensnare one person after another, and I hope that by pointing them out, they won't ensnare you.

Chapter 5

Becoming the King Before You Put on the Crown

Vladimir: Well? What do we do?

Estragon: Don't let's do anything. It's safer.

Vladimir: Let's wait and see what he says.

Estragon: Who?

Vladimir: Godot.

Estragon: Good idea.

Vladimir: Let's wait till we know exactly how we stand.

Estragon: On the other hand it might be better to strike the iron before it freezes.

Vladimir: I'm curious to hear what he has to offer. Then we'll take it or leave it.

Estragon: What exactly did we ask him for?

—from Samuel Beckett's *Waiting for Godot*

As I was growing up, a framed picture of a duck on a placid lake in autumn hung on the wall of my bedroom. Under the duck and sort of in the water was the familiar scripture Jeremiah 29:11: "'For I know the plans I have for you,' declares the LORD, 'plans to prosper you and not to harm you, plans to give you hope and a future.'" I took hope in that promise as a child, and I still do, for it is a pledge from God that our calling is sure. But the great and less commonly recognized thing about this verse is that, like so many others, there is more to the message. This famous promise is the culmination of a process delineated in the preceding verses, and this process gives full meaning and significance to the promise.

I love the prophet Jeremiah because he was so passionate and gritty and raw. For about half of his book, his eyes flowed with rivers of tears because of the waywardness and the impending destruction of his people. Then it happened. Everything he had been prophesying came to pass: The Babylonian war machine under the leadership of King Nebuchadnezzar breached the walls of Jerusalem, the invaders overwhelmed the defending army, and the city fell. The horror that followed—the devastation of the Israelite's homeland, the mass murder of their countrymen, and harsh subjugation in exile for the survivors—doubtless intensified the people's quest for hope and their eager longing for the fulfillment of God's good design. Jeremiah's words in chapter 29—"To the surviving elders among the exiles and to the priests, the prophets and all the other people Nebuchadnezzar had carried into exile from Jerusalem to Babylon"[1]—are full of hope and the reassurance of God's faithfulness, and by these words the remnant of Israel was surely comforted and encouraged. But Jeremiah's letter provides more than just the reassurance that the calling of God on our lives still stands. It is a blueprint for getting from here to there—a strategic plan for living into the calling.

Even though you don't get a wrong understanding of Jeremiah 29:11 when you read the verse in isolation, it is interesting to note that every major translation of this passage begins with the conjunction *for.* The word in the Hebrew text is *kiy* (pronounced "kee"), which, according to *Strong's Exhaustive Concordance of the Bible,* "indicates causal relations of all kinds, antecedent or consequent." That means the statement following this word is true because of the preceding ideas; it is a consequence of them. What precedes verse 11 is a list of instructions on living, as it were, in the meantime. It is as if God were saying, "Do these things that I am telling you now, while you are waiting on the fulfillment of my promise to bring you back from exile and restore your prosperity and joy, because I know the plans I have for you." In other words, "I have plans for you, they are sure, you are called. Therefore, live this way. This is how I would like you to wait."

Look at those verses:

> This is what the LORD Almighty, the God of Israel, says to all those I carried into exile from Jerusalem to Babylon: "Build houses and settle down; plant gardens and eat what they produce. Marry and have sons and daughters; find wives for your sons and give your daughters in marriage, so that they too may have sons and daughters. Increase in number there; do not decrease. Also, seek the peace and prosperity of the city to which I have carried you into exile. Pray to the LORD for it, because if it prospers, you too will prosper." Yes, this is what the LORD Almighty, the God of Israel, says: "Do not let the prophets and diviners among you

> deceive you. Do not listen to the dreams you encourage them to have. They are prophesying lies to you in my name. I have not sent them," declares the LORD.
>
> This is what the LORD says: "When seventy years are completed for Babylon, I will come to you and fulfill my gracious promise to bring you back to this place. For I know the plans I have for you," declares the LORD, "plans to prosper you and not to harm you, plans to give you hope and a future."[2]

Notice the big idea: "While you are waiting on me, do stuff. Be proactive. Don't cloister yourself and put life on hold in anticipation of a divine override. Heed the road I've pointed out for you and live robustly along that road into the calling. Do the work along the way. Take your eyes off yourself and take care of other people. Press into my heart. And then, one day, one unannounced and deeply longed-for day, you'll wake up and find that what you have looked toward and longed for has all come to pass. Do these things as I have said, because my plans for you are sure and better than you can even imagine."

God's Idea of Waiting

In these verses in Jeremiah 29, God gave his people specific and pragmatic guidance for constructive, effective waiting—waiting that yields results. God's idea is *proactive* waiting: trusting, seeking, and looking to him for the dream's fulfillment while we seek to grow, stretch, and forge usable tools for the future from the raw iron of life's unalterable seasons. As we do the stuff of life with the same vigor with which we cling to the dream God has given us, we'll find ourselves growing ever more useful to him.

Let's take a closer look at God's instructions to his people.

"Build houses and settle down." During the season of waiting, establish yourself. Know that the waiting is not your ultimate home, and resist the inclination to despise the season of becoming. God's provision, protection, and blessing are available to you now, just as they will be when you arrive at your final destination, so pursue them and trust in them. Instead of wandering, *be* in the time of waiting and embrace it. Be productive and create something of worth for the kingdom of God.

It is amazing to me how many people think that building while waiting is bad. Don't think that what you build now has to be your magnum opus, your life's crowning achievement. Just build what you can. The important thing is to stop sitting around waiting for God to sprinkle the calling dust on your head or looking for an angel to descend and tap you with the fulfillment wand. It's not going to happen, so you might as well get started building something of value and producing something that is useful.

God instructed the exiles, who were eagerly awaiting his deliverance, to build houses where they were. Most of us have a dream house in mind, but few can afford to build that home in our twenties or thirties. Does that mean we shouldn't buy a house at all, since we can't yet have the one we ultimately want? Of course not! You know the drill—you buy what you can, build equity, and move up. Never to buy that first house out of principle—hey, this is not my long-term home, so forget it!—is often foolish and leads to a depressing life of six-month leases and noisy upstairs neighbors. God's idea is for you to establish a baseline by starting to build now.

"Plant gardens and eat what they produce." Next, God instructed his exiled and anxiously waiting people to plant a crop that would yield abundant returns. In the parable of the talents, Jesus spoke of the rewards

given to the two servants who took what little they had—an amount far from their dreams, it's safe to assume—and generated more. To each man the master said, "Well done, good and faithful servant! You have been faithful with a few things; I will put you in charge of many things. Come and share your master's happiness!"[3] Each servant found his ultimate fulfillment, it seems—or at least took measurable strides toward it—in proportion to what he produced while he waited. The one who produced nothing waited foolishly, and even what he had was taken from him.

The impulse to do nothing of value until you live into your calling is strong—this is the way of the super-spiritualizer—but you must overcome it. Know that God is sure of his plans for you. Therefore, settle down, establish yourself, and start producing something.

"Marry and have sons and daughters.... Increase in number there; do not decrease." Do the things of life along the way. *There*—in the season of receiving, dreaming, and waiting—we are to increase. Again, it is tempting and seems spiritual to stall, stop, and stay as we are while we wait on the Lord. We will start increasing when the vision becomes clear and real, we reason. The trouble with this is that God's design is just the opposite: He wants us to grow, stretch, and increase in number and influence *while we are here,* not once we are there. Opportunities to strengthen our lives abound as we walk through life faithfully serving God; we need to seize them.

"Seek the peace and prosperity of the city to which I have carried you into exile. Pray to the LORD for it, because if it prospers, you too will prosper." Bad waiting brings with it a subtle whisper telling us it's fine—even noble, under the banner of not casting our pearls before swine—if we slack in our precalling roles. What a shame that I can readily think of dozens of young men and women who've informed me passionately of their zeal to get on with their callings but who I know are doing shoddy work in their

current jobs. This just won't fly! You can count on it—these people will be doubly frustrated. First, because their dreams never seem to become reality, and second, because they are miserable and unsuccessful in their perpetual predream season. Proactive waiting means doing a great job *now,* hitting the ball out of the park, doing all the work we find to do before the dream becomes reality.

"Do not let the prophets and diviners among you deceive you. Do not listen to the dreams you encourage them to have." Most of us say whatever we think others want to hear. It's in our nature to do it, so we can expect others to do it as well. People will give us all kinds of foolish advice, such as "Follow your heart" and "You are the architect of your destiny." Don't listen to them. Stay the course of God's call, learn to hear the Shepherd's voice, and listen to him above all. Proactive waiting means vigilantly rejecting the bad ideas that flood your mind and clinging to God's design. It's worth noting that super-spiritualizers can never, it seems, get enough super-spirituality. Perhaps to justify their own sloth, they seem bent on persuading others of the virtue of *really* listening to God and not doing anything without his expressed, written, miracle-validated consent. Don't listen to them. Don't get sucked into that whirlpool. Stay steady, embrace God's idea of waiting, and watch him easily accomplish in your life what others struggle to bring about by their own efforts.

Live into the Calling

The challenge David faced after Samuel anointed him and left is the challenge that faces us as we live into the calling that has become so precious to us: to figure out what it looks like, practically speaking, to wait on the Lord. I came home from the life-changing summer in Africa radically redirected, and it fell to me to figure out, *Where, precisely, do I go from here?* I was increasingly sure that God had called me to be a pastor, which answered one question (What exactly am I supposed to do?) and raised a new one (How do I get there from here?) What I was essentially asking was, *What do I do while I wait?* If God had called me to pastor, and if I stayed faithful to him, then I would ultimately pastor. But the question of what to do along the way remained.

So one day I made this choice, which in turn made *me* for the ensuing decade: If God had called me to pastor someday, then I would live like a pastor now. And that's what I set out to do. By day I was another engineering student ("enginerds," as the philosophy majors, who always seemed to have plenty of time for twirling sticks and tossing Frisbees in the quad, were fond of calling us), but by night I was pastor-boy. I realized that I was pursuing the calling, not the job, and it made no sense to live as if a résumé would someday secure a pastoral position.

Even in my youthful naiveté, I knew better than to assume that I could continue to live the life of a student/church member/nice guy who tried to resist my sin impulses and treat people well and then—all because, in East Africa, I sensed God calling me to a ministry career—God would one day decide to wave his calling wand or sprinkle me with the magic pixie dust of destiny and—*poof!*—turn me into a pastor. It became clear to me in the months after my trip to Africa, just as it must have become clear to David in the days and weeks following Samuel's visit, that God had put the calling before me and given me the choice to start walking into it.

In retrospect, I smile to think that I viewed myself not unlike the Greatest American Hero: an ordinary, slightly nerdy, and sometimes unsure twentysomething, trying to make his way in the world by day, and a specially empowered crusader of goodness and virtue (minus the tight and colorful suit) by night. I supposed that, for a reason unknown to me,

I had been the recipient of some grand mission that was as unclear as it was unexpected, and I concluded that there would be no green flag or starting gun or gala reception. There was nothing, really—only the impulse to start living into the calling and wait for further instructions. The same was true for the Greatest American Hero: No one told him to begin; it was just time. Whatever would come of his destiny, he would have a swashbuckling, unorthodox, but forward-moving start on which to build.

Here's what that meant for me: As a twenty-year-old college junior, I decided to begin living the calling God had revealed. I began to study the Bible the way a pastor would study the Bible, to pray the way a pastor ought to pray, and to love people the way a pastor is charged with loving people. Some are inclined to believe that one is a pastor because he stands on a platform and preaches, his name and title appear on a church-office door, and he receives his paycheck every month from the tithes and offerings of his congregation. Others believe that one is a leader solely because of his rank, position, or title. But in my military leadership training, I learned that a leader isn't necessarily the one with the title; a leader is the one people follow. A pastor of seminary degrees, titles, and positions can be produced through years of training and experience, but the process of making a pastor whom God uses to change lives begins long before any of those achievements.

My life changed irreversibly that fall after East Africa. I don't mean "changed" in the theoretical sense, as in *what my life stood for changed.* I mean that my life changed in the most practical ways, like how I spent my time and money. Some of the alterations were gradual, and others were abrupt. Some were well received by my friends, and others gave them pause. But all of the changes were measurable and fairly drastic and, taken together, holistic. They reflect who I am, and I want to tell you about them. The stories about these changes are instructive and embarrassing and funny and real, and they will lace the chapters that follow.

The Evolution of a Calling

Reflection has a way of bringing clarity. Not one part of the process of the past twelve years of my life makes sense in terms of traditional pastoral training, but when all the pieces are viewed together, it is obvious that God was directing things—me—according to his perfect plan. In retrospect I've seen that God's calling is far more in the process than in the product. Here's what I mean: I've lived most of my life with the notion that God's calling is an event or a position or an achievement—some high rung on the ladder that, after many years of obligatory climbing, we hope someday to attain. On the contrary, the past twelve years have taught me that the calling evolves.

(I know. The word *evolve* is something of a taboo for Christians. It's like talking about Hitler—not only can't you say he was good, but you also can't say anything good about him. For example, you can't say Hitler had strong leadership qualities or was a nice dresser or had a cute dog. Bill Clinton is kind of like this in our camp. Two months ago I was chastised in an e-mail from a disgruntled congregant after saying in a sermon illustration that, in my view, Bill Clinton was a fiscally responsible president. Of course, I don't expect everyone to agree with my opinions, and in this instance, my critic's near-apoplectic protestations had to do not with my opinion but with the *premise* behind it. She felt—and stated in several paragraphs of choice words—that no believer who is truly washed in the blood of the Lord Jesus, and least of all a preacher, who, she reminded me, would be judged more strictly, could possibly say anything positive about Bill Clinton. Needless to say, I was baffled. Likewise, saying among Christians that anything *evolves* can be harrowing for a pastor because of the looks you get and the comments you know will be coming your way in an e-mail in a couple of days.)

Nonetheless, I stand by my statement: Your calling *evolves.* It evolves the way love evolves, as a product of your experiences along the way, the thousand mundane daily choices to serve your spouse, to prefer her needs to your own, to live each day for her good. That's why my Grandmother and Granddaddy Southerland, who were married fifty years, could stand up at the family reunion/anniversary celebration in honor of their stat-defying longevity as a couple and say that they love each other more now than ever before. It's simple, really—the great mystery of love. For what is love but to subordinate oneself to another? It follows, then, that what began as mutual attraction and the enjoyment of each other's personalities evolved into this "many-splendored thing" of years and lives and small daily decisions.

I have concluded that we never arrive at our calling; we only live into it. We never get there, and when we think we do, we invariably learn sooner or later that what we thought was the end is really just another beginning. You may recall from math class that a line segment is a connection of two points. Like this:

•——————————————————•

In our early years we may think of the moment we heard from God as the *origin* and the living out of our calling as the *terminus.* But I have discovered over the past decade that our calling isn't the terminus; it's the line. We tend to view so much of our lives as the process of getting to the calling. But that's just the thing: The process *is* the calling. The calling of God is the path, the walk of obedience through the seasons of life. God is much more interested in the process than the product.

That is why David's early years are to me the most interesting. He heard God's direction—"You will be king"—and then spent the next several years living into the calling. David the king was a product of David the teenage shepherd, David the courier, David the court musician, David the armor bearer, David the unlikely hero, and David the fugitive. He spent those instrumental years becoming the king long before he ever put on the crown. He spent those years growing up, figuring out God, choosing who to be. He spent those years cultivating his calling, and history's greatest king was the result. David made a series of decisions along the way, most of them mundane and matter-of-course, and those decisions decided his legacy. It is to those mundane, life-shaping, world-changing decisions that we turn our focus.

Chapter 6

Thriving Under Authority

"What you been doing in there?"

"Nothing."

"Nothing! Look at your hands. And look at your mouth. What is that truck?"

"I don't know, aunt."

"Well, I know. It's jam—that's what it is. Forty times I've said if you didn't let that jam alone I'd skin you. Hand me that switch."

The switch hovered in the air—the peril was desperate—

"My! Look behind you, aunt!"

The old lady whirled round, and snatched her skirts out of danger. The lad fled, on the instant, scrambled up the high board fence, and disappeared over it.

—MARK TWAIN, from *Tom Sawyer*

For Jesse's youngest son, life continued to be painfully normal for some time after the prophet visited the tribe of Benjamin and turned David's world upside down. But now—knowing what he knew, being who he was—everything was different. After once getting a glance down the long bright hallway of his calling, how exactly was he to go back to watching over a pasture full of sheep? The choice arrested him daily: Do you push the calling, force it, do something to make it happen—or wait? How do you wait for something like this? Hours seem like years, weeks like decades. The fancy idea of being king rose and fell with each new day, wandering around in his mind like sheep on a hill.

Then one day, just when, for the thousandth time, the burden of knowing and not knowing what to do about it became unbearable:

> Saul's attendants said to [Saul], "See, an evil spirit from God is tormenting you. Let our lord command his servants here to search for someone who can play the harp. He will play when the evil spirit from God comes upon you, and you will feel better."
>
> So Saul said to his attendants, "Find someone who plays well and bring him to me."
>
> One of the servants answered, "I have seen a son of Jesse of Bethlehem who knows how to play the harp. He is a brave man and a warrior. He speaks well and is a fine-looking man. And the LORD is with him."
>
> Then Saul sent messengers to Jesse and said, "Send me your son David, who is with the sheep."[1]

This is it! Naturally, I just needed to wait awhile, grow up a little bit, and then, at just the right time, the king sends for me! David, welcome to the rest of your life...

So David left the pasture to serve King Saul's demon-soothing needs, and as the Bible records, "Saul liked him very much, and David became one of his armor-bearers. Then Saul sent word to Jesse, saying, 'Allow David to remain in my service, for I am pleased with him.'"[2] We might be inclined to think that Jesse said, "Sure, keep him in your service, O King," but the Scriptures suggest otherwise. Later the text adds, "The three oldest [of David's brothers] followed Saul, but David went back and forth from Saul to tend his father's sheep at Bethlehem."[3]

Now think about that. David got the nod from Samuel, started to visualize his calling, waited around the family ranch in eager anticipation for months, maybe years, stayed steady in his work and faithful to his God, and then—finally!—the palace calls. You can imagine that David thought this was it: *Bye-bye sheep; I'm outta here! God spoke back then, left me to put in my obligatory time in the desert, and now his sovereign plan is unfolding.* Like Luke Skywalker blasting his way out of Mos Eisley with Obi-Wan, Han, and the droids to save Princess Leia, free the galaxy from the oppressive Imperial forces, and break Darth Vader's despotic stranglehold, this was good-bye provincial farm boy of obscurity and hello destiny! You have to believe that, in his mind, David was never going back.

Things got better for David in a hurry. Life in the palace was a new and wonderful world of sophisticated people, fine food, and fabulous treatment. It didn't take long for provincial shepherd life to fade to a speck in the rearview mirror of David's consciousness, and then disappear altogether. Armed with a skill that was vital to King Saul and with a newly fortified assurance of his royal destiny, David embraced his new life with all the vigor of a kid who has headed off to college and left home and boyhood forever.

So now picture the horror: David was living in the palace with King Saul, doing a good job with his demon-soothing responsibilities, being embraced by the senior staff, and getting promoted to the coveted post of armor bearer. By every account, David was off to the races. You can picture him strutting around the palace like Simba the young lion king and heir-apparent, shoulders back and chest out, singing "I just can't wait to be king." Then one alarming day: "David, phone's for you."

"Hello?"

"David, it's your father—"

"*Dad!!* I can't believe you're calling me here! How embarrassing…"

"Yeaaahhh… Listen, David, I'm going to need you to come home and help with the sheep."

A Painful Decision

David now faced a core life decision. It seems minor in the scriptural account and to our modern sensibilities, but in the process of David's living into his calling it's a landmark moment, a watershed event. I'll tell you why. At this point in David's life, God allowed him to choose how he was going to respond to authority. Let's face it; David didn't have to go back home. Six months ago obedience to his father was compulsory, as it is for each of us when we are growing up in our parents' home. You remember: "Not as long as you live under *my* roof and *I* put food on the table for you…" (That was, I think, my father's exact response when, at age sixteen, I wanted to drive down to New York City from our suburban Boston town to attend a Grateful Dead concert. His words were perhaps followed by: "No way! Not as long as I draw the breath of life!" I remember thinking that I would have to pry the car keys from the steely grip of his cold, lifeless fingers before that trip was ever going to happen.)

But David didn't need his father's provision or protection any longer. Dad wasn't paying his tuition or car insurance, and David wasn't living off Dad's credit card. David was on his own and doing fine. Plus, we already know that Saul wanted Jesse to let David stay in the king's service, and since David's arrival, the king had only become more and more pleased with the young man's work. At this point, David was certainly old enough to be out on his own. And, for goodness sake, going back to the sheep would have been a major step in the wrong direction! After all, hadn't God called him to be king? Hadn't his patience in the wilderness of waiting brought him to this next step in the process of living into his calling? And wasn't he now in the very place kings live? No, it made no sense at all to go home now.

To make the decision even harder, war was breaking out. All during the time David had been in Saul's service, tensions had continued to mount between Israel and its neighbor and archenemy, the Philistines. Now tension had escalated to hostility and, inevitably, war. War! Now this is where kings are made…on the battlefield! Demon-soothing is fine—it's a foot in the door—but this is a real opportunity. War. That great maker of kings and heroes that had characterized Israel's relationship with the Philistines as long as David had been alive was once again summoning the strong and brave to the field of battle. *This is it! This is my chance! I've killed my lions and bears, and I can kill Philistines just the same. At last the journey begins. This is my hour! Good-bye, harp boy…here comes King David!*

Ironically, this same war—and specifically the summons for Israel's young and strong to serve in King Saul's conscript army—created the need for David to go back home. The war took Jesse's older boys from him and left him needing help with the family business. First Samuel 17:13-14 tells us, "Jesse's three oldest sons had followed Saul to the war.... David was the youngest." David had the experience, he was reliable, he was available, and he was presumably beneath the standard age of military service. So it's not that David's father was being sadistic or jealous by yanking his son out of his posh setup. Surely he didn't want to hinder David's advancement in his calling; he just needed help. Jesse's request of his youngest son was innocent and legitimate, but it was in reality unenforceable. It was just a request.

So David had a decision to make. One step forward or two steps back—it was his choice. Honor his father and miss this great opportunity, or seize the moment and charge ahead in the name of the calling. It had to be tempting for David to manhandle the plans at this point. It would have been so easy, so natural, to force this thing forward. And the most alluring part is it could all have been done in God-garb—justified as fearing and obeying God, no matter what the cost. (I mean, hey, didn't Jesus say that unless a follower hates his father and mother, he cannot be a disciple?[4]) There were loads of pseudospiritual justifications here for doing what he wanted to do.

But David didn't. The Bible tells us, "The three oldest [of Jesse's sons] followed Saul, but David went back and forth from Saul to tend his father's sheep at Bethlehem."[5] The war was raging. David's brothers were fighting. Saul's armor doubtless required full-time bearing. But David honored his father, and I believe his decision laid a foundation for the many hard years that were to come. He chose to submit to God's authority, and this choice positioned him for a future of radical blessings that come only to those who demonstrate their trustworthiness to God.

Understanding the Government of God

One of the few things I remember from my junior-high Latin class is a phrase used mainly by lawyers and literary scholars: *sine qua non.* For some reason it stuck with me all these years. Literally translated, the term means "without which not." It is the indispensable element, the core component, that which, if absent, causes the whole structure to come crashing down around you. It is the keystone of an arch, the carbonation in a soda, the engine in a car.

With respect to living into your calling in Christ, responding well to authority is the sine qua non. Sadly, over the years I have seen a number of talented people spin their wheels and never get traction because they are not willing to submit to God's delegated authority in their lives. You can be the brightest, most articulate, or most socially skilled person on the planet, and you'll still find yourself struggling to find the road of your calling if you do not learn to submit to God's delegated authority. His authority is the entrance to your calling.

To get your mind around the idea of God's delegated authority, it's important to understand the way his dominion operates. God's kingdom is steadily advancing on the earth, and with it, his government. His plans, purposes, and ideas concerning the events of human history are being worked out as his kingdom is displacing the "god of this age."[6] Jesus told us, "From the days of John the Baptist until now, the kingdom of heaven has been forcefully advancing,"[7] and Isaiah added concerning the age of Christ, "Of the increase of his government…there will be no end."[8] Jesus taught that the kingdom of God is manifested primarily in the hearts of those who trust him for salvation. So, in short, the kingdom and, consequently, the government of God take root and grow on the earth as people yield their lives in totality to him. Okay, so that's Kingdom of God 101.

We may talk and read a lot about God's kingdom, but how exactly are we to understand the idea of his *government?* Dictionary.com defines *government* as "the exercise of authority in a political unit; rule." In effect, government is the manner or system a ruler employs to carry out his authority in the lives of the people in his charge. So God's government is the way he implements his leadership. Our senior pastor delegates his authority to members of his staff regarding the affairs of the church so that the worship pastor is empowered to make decisions about the music, the youth pastor has the authority to make decisions about the ministry to teens, and so on. It's not that our senior pastor gives up his authority, but rather he finds it most efficient to express it through his trusted surrogates. That is basically how God's government on earth works.

There are four channels through which God delegates authority in our lives: the home, the workplace, the government, and the church. Each line of God's delegated authority is empowered by the Creator with particular responsibilities for maintaining order, ensuring our safety and protection, and enabling the flow of his blessing in our lives. When we align ourselves rightly within God's authority system, what we are actually doing is appropriating the kingdom of God in our lives.

Appropriating the Kingdom

We all know that the war is on—for our culture, our families, our own souls—and that the Enemy is prowling around "looking for someone to devour."[9] Jesus knew that the reality of the clash of kingdoms would characterize the plight of the New Testament church, and so he taught his followers to pray, "Thy kingdom come. Thy will be done in earth, as it is in heaven."[10] Jesus gave us this prayer precisely because he knew that the Enemy's kingdom would continue pressing hard to take ground; he knew that to accomplish the mission for which the Father had sent him to earth, the kingdom of God had to press harder. This happens when Christ's followers *appropriate* the kingdom, just the way Congress's various committees appropriate to the various departments and projects the funds made available by the taxpayers.

How do we appropriate the kingdom? By praying for it, establishing it in our praises, availing ourselves of it by dying to our flesh and choosing a lifestyle of holiness, and to the point here, submitting to God's delegated authority in our lives. When we submit to authority in each of its prescribed lines, we solidify God's government. It's no different from a developing nation's choice to submit to popularly elected, term-limited, internationally legitimized government regimes that exist to serve the people. When democracy first gains footing in a country, the defeated ruling party is often reluctant to relinquish power, and the tyranny-weary populace fears that a regime change will lead to further exploitation and oppression. But with time, their confidence in democracy grows, and they more readily submit to the governing authority. What that collective submission does is to ratify, substantiate, and strengthen good governance. And that is precisely what happens when we submit to God's authority: We ratify his good governance in our lives and further substantiate the reign of his kingdom on earth.

This is all great news for the global cause of Christ, for which we are all naturally advocates, but what does it mean for us individually? You may have heard submission to authority likened to an umbrella, and so it is. But I prefer to think of it as a shield. Because we live in a world that is fallen, sinful, and bound over to the temporary governing authority of the Enemy of our souls, we are subject to the forces that operate in the world. I know it seems that as believers in Christ, we should be immune to the negative effects of living in a world that is subject to the perils of natural law, the evil designs of Satan, and the consequences of bad ideas and decisions. But it's just not true. I know, I know. Many of us grew up in churches that taught that believers are totally exempt from the throes of illness, the attacks of evil spirits, and the madness of people like Osama bin Laden, if only we can activate our faith. But this is wrong. What those well-intentioned teachers inevitably fail to explain is why no one *does* live that way. Does none of us have the faith? Nowhere does the Bible promise that we will be exempt from the consequences of living in a fallen world; in fact, it assures us that those who follow Christ will meet with persecution and struggle.[11]

Just as God loves us and has a wonderful plan for our lives, Satan hates us and has a plan for our destruction. You can imagine the Enemy on the field of battle, firing arrows at you in steady volleys with great precision. Now you are behind a great shield, against which the Enemy's arrows have no effect; they bounce right off the shield and fall harmlessly to the ground. That is just what submission to God's authority does in our lives: It facilitates God's blessings and thwarts the Enemy's best-laid plans for our destruction. But if we step out from behind the shield, it's open season. Rebellion is a sure step down the path of frustration, disappointment, and, ultimately, destruction.

Here's another way of looking at it: When we align ourselves with God's government, we enjoy the benefits of citizenship in his kingdom. Just as law-abiding, tax-paying Americans enjoy the rightful protection of law enforcement and our armed services as benefits of American citizenship, we who submit to God's government enjoy the protection of God's ramparts, watchtowers, and armaments as benefits of being citizens in his kingdom.

Now, let's turn to an in-depth discussion of the delegated authority that God has established for our protection and blessing.

The Four Lines of Delegated Authority

1. Home

Ephesians 5 teaches that Christ is the head of the church, and in like manner, the husband is the head of his wife (and, by deduction, the rest of his family).[12] So if you were to trace the progression of authority, it would pass from Christ to the husband, then from the husband to the wife, and then from the husband and wife to the children. At the time of creation, God established—and Christ later affirmed—that marriage is the trigger point for the shift in home authority: "a man will leave his father and mother and be united to his wife, and they will become one flesh."[13] At the wedding, each party leaves one line of God's delegated authority and realigns under a new chain of command—the husband answers directly to Christ, and the new wife submits to her husband. Until the time of marriage, though, there is no scriptural reason to believe that we are at some arbitrary point released from our parents' God-given authority, and many people need to get this right.

I frequently meet with young single adults who tell me what a hindrance their parents are to their lives. Many of us become persuaded in our teens or young-adult years that our parents' rightful influence ceases at some age: sixteen, I've heard, because you can drive (a scary thought in itself, and thank God there's not a chance that's true!); eighteen, many more have said, because you are legally an adult (remember, civil government is instituted by God; not the reverse); twenty-one, others have suggested, because, I suppose, you can buy alcohol (exactly the time in many young people's lives when they most need a good whippin' with Daddy's belt!); twenty-five, for what possible reason I can't imagine, except, perhaps, that you can rent a car in California. On and on the arguments have gone, always attempting to do one thing, and that is to justify rebellion.

No, my friend, there is no getting out of it. You can theorize and pontificate and wax philosophic until you've convinced all your friends, but it's just never going to be true. Listen to me, my single, twenty-seven-year-old, haven't-lived-with-your-parents-in-nine-years reader—you *are* still under your parents' authority according to God. I know this is objectionable to many of you because I have listened to the vehement protestations over many a caramel macchiato, but it's just the way it is. You may want to go ahead and begin getting used to it because it seems unlikely that God is going to change his mind on this one.

It is worth pointing out, just as the apostle Paul did, that the injunction to honor our parents is the first commandment with a promise: "that it may go well with you and that you may enjoy long life on the earth."[14] Tremendous blessing is available to us when we actively acknowledge God's delegated authority through our parents. It periodically amazes me that young adults forfeit much of the very blessing they seek by prematurely withdrawing themselves from their parents' authority.

2. Workplace

Paul's instructions concerning slaves and masters have confounded many in the church. His words find their truest application here. In Ephesians 6:5, Paul wrote, "Slaves, obey your earthly masters with respect and fear, and with sincerity of heart, just as you would obey Christ." Many of us balk at this idea because it seems to endorse slavery. But the Bible no more condones slavery here than it condones bad parenting in the passage we looked at previously. The purpose of this passage is not socio-economic commentary but personal instruction. The big idea here is:

Whether the exercise of authority in your workplace is just or unjust, submit. The passage in Ephesians continues: "[Serve] with enthusiasm, as though you were [serving] the Lord rather than...people. Remember that the Lord will reward each one of us for the good we do, whether we are slaves or free."[15] As with God's delegated authority in the home, we are blessed when we recognize that in submitting to our workplace authority, we are, in fact, submitting to Christ.

Way too often I talk to people who are zealous for the advent of God's calling in their lives but are doing pathetic work in their current place of employment. Their thinking, I suppose, is that God has bigger things in store for them than this petty job. Frequently they will tell me how they are suffering persecution at work at the hands of a godless tyrant who expects them to flip burgers all day and doesn't respect their need to read their Bibles frequently during their shift. To stay at that job and work hard for that person, the reasoning goes, would be casting pearls before swine. Here's the problem with that reasoning: It's entirely wrong. First, flipping burgers (or insert your own current not-my-calling job—waiting tables, filing papers, designing buildings, fabricating microchips, whatever) is the job you were hired to do. A boss's expectation that you in fact do it, however disdainful to your recently refined spiritual sensibilities, is not persecution. It's capitalism, it's integrity, and it is good. Furthermore, a boss's lack of interest in your ultimate calling and especially in its being fulfilled in his workplace while you are on the clock is perfectly sensible.

And, finally, even if you are genuinely being persecuted in your workplace, you must still submit to the one in authority over you as unto the Lord. This is a major violation of our twenty-first-century American expectation of absolute fairness above everything else, but it is quite consistent with God's expectation. The apostle Peter wrote, "Submit yourselves to your masters with all respect, not only to those who are good and considerate, *but also to those who are harsh.* For it is commendable if a man bears up under the pain of unjust suffering because he is conscious of God." We are not submitting to God's authority if we slack on the job, complain about the boss, and quit without two weeks' notice because we were treated poorly. The passage continues, "How is it to your credit if you receive a beating for doing wrong and endure it?" which suggests that lackadaisical Christian workers often deserve harsh treatment. "But if you suffer for doing good and you endure it, this is commendable before God." Notice this: "*To this you were called,* because Christ suffered for you, leaving you an example, that you should follow in his steps."[16] Not only is being treated unfairly at work not necessarily an impediment to our calling that justifies poor performance, but it is actually part of our calling! Model Jesus's humility and selflessness by submitting to his delegated authority in the workplace and excelling—no matter what the work, when the hours, or who the boss—and find yourself thriving in the process of living into your calling.

I have a good friend who is an assistant manager at a popular retail clothing store. He told me that when hiring new employees, his manager is hesitant when an applicant indicates that he or she is a Christian. The reason she hesitates? "Christian kids don't work as hard, and they want more concessions." (Come to think of it, I have to confess that in the same way, if I'm brutally honest, I am a little hesitant when I'm looking for a contractor or service provider for our home and see a little fish symbol on the corner of the advertisement.) It's sad and shameful that Christ's followers have even the slightest such stigma. We who are called by God ought to be the hardest working, the most punctual, the most reliable, and the most valuable workers in every corner of the marketplace—no matter what we perceive our ultimate calling to be. If we don't get authority right, our calling will always be just some lofty, unattainable dream.

3. Government

In Romans 13, Paul wrote,

> Everyone must submit himself to the governing authorities, for there is no authority except that which God has established. The authorities that exist have been established by God. Consequently, he who rebels against the authority is rebelling against what God has instituted, and those who do so will bring judgment on themselves.[17]

Many Christians I meet with—particularly those who view the end times as imminent—harbor a shocking disdain for governmental authority. Those who chronically expect the Antichrist to take the form of a handsome, articulate Democrat, who bemoaned the government's ending of the gold standard as the next step down the road toward the mark-of-the-beast microchip being inserted under our skin, and who perpetually suspect the nefarious secret dealings of the Illuminati seem to be most susceptible to this violation. Of course, we must be vigilant and wary in anticipation of the thief-in-the-night unfolding of events during the end times. But nothing—not end-times vigilance or disagreement with public policy or the impassioned rants of civil-disobedience-preaching Christian personalities—justifies rebellion against government authorities.

I know a Christian couple who talk openly and persuasively about the fact that they have not paid federal income tax for years. The federal income tax is not constitutional, they maintain, and therefore it is optional. This confounds me. Where in the U.S. Constitution does it afford us the responsibility or right to interpret the Constitution? That, it seems, is the role of the judiciary. And doesn't federal law mandate taxes? So, in effect, what these folks have done is to say, "We feel we know better than the collective body of our elected legislators what the law should be, and we feel we know better than the whole judicial branch what the Constitution really says, and so we're not going to obey the law *on principle*." That's not principle at all! It's flagrant, juvenile disobedience. It's no surprise to me that this family has struggled financially as long as I have known them.

This is the way many of us respond to God's delegated authority. If we like what it has to say, we follow it. If not, we disregard it and come up with some gross spiritual justification for our disobedience and withdraw ourselves from the blessing and protection of God's government, all the while defaming the name of Christ.

4. Church

Scripture recounts Paul's submission to the authority of the church in Jerusalem over an issue of doctrine that was critical to the expansion of the gospel. According to the book of Acts,

> Some men came down from Judea to Antioch and were teaching the brothers: "Unless you are circumcised, according to the custom taught by Moses, you cannot be saved." This brought Paul and Barnabas into sharp dispute and debate with them. So Paul and Barnabas were appointed, along with some other believers, to go up to Jerusalem.[18]

According to the biblical account, the apostles and elders gathered to discuss the issue. Different ones expressed opinions, and in the end, James made a decision:

> It is my judgment…that we should not make it difficult for the Gentiles who are turning to God. Instead we should write to them, telling them to abstain from food polluted by idols, from sexual immorality, from the meat of strangled animals and from blood. For Moses has been preached in every city from the earliest times and is read in the synagogues on every Sabbath.[19]

Churches have different understandings of their authority over the lives of their congregants. It's important to choose a church with which you agree on this subject—and then choose to submit to its authority. The church gives us a framework for understanding Scripture, relating to God, and connecting with other people. Too many of us participate in a local church on our terms; we attend when we feel like it, participate how we want to, and pick and choose the teachings we want to follow. As we live into our calling, it's vital that we find a strong, healthy church and plug in. And then stay put.

I remember when I started attending New Life Church. I quickly became persuaded that the leadership was godly, the doctrine was sound, and the vision was in line with the heart of God. As I attended services, I heard our pastor tell the congregation again and again that we weren't meant to follow Christ alone, that we were designed to be in life-giving relationships with other people, and that the best way to facilitate those relationships was to get involved in a small group. I didn't have to subject this teaching to critical analysis. I felt no compulsion to go to the Greek and make sure that the pastor was accurately exegeting the subtle implications of the text. It was apparent to me that what he was encouraging us to do was not heretical, and it was the way to thrive in that church, so I just did it. I looked in the small-group directory, found a group for single young adults, and started participating in the meetings and activities. While my going to "the X-Change" was a relatively simple act of submission, it yielded huge blessings in my life: I met my wife; I met the pastor who became a mentor, then a dear friend, and then the chief proponent of my being hired years later; I earned the trust of lots of wonderful friends, whom I still treasure today; and I got the privilege, a little while later, of branching off and leading my own small group.

■ ■ ■

Too often we think of all the reasons why we should not submit to authority. It's easy to focus on the weaknesses, inconsistencies, and errors of anyone in leadership—those things are always there to be found. And I'm not suggesting you check your brain at the door and mindlessly do whatever anyone says. Somewhere short of drinking the red Kool-Aid, though, is a wonderful place of loving, believing in, serving—and, yes, submitting to—God's delegated authority. I encourage you to find that place, because it is an indispensable step on the road to your calling. It's the sine qua non.

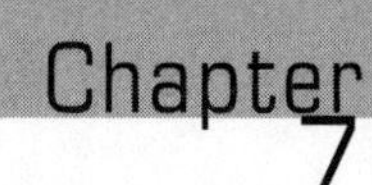

Chapter 7

Kill Your Lions and Bears

Battle Commander: The approach will not be easy. You are required to maneuver straight down this trench and skim the surface to this point. The target area is only two meters wide. It's a small thermal exhaust port, right below the main port. The shaft leads directly to the reactor system. A precise hit will start a chain reaction which should destroy the station.

[A murmur of disbelief runs through the room.]

Commander: Only a precise hit will set up a chain reaction. The shaft is ray-shielded, so you'll have to use proton torpedoes.

Wedge: That's impossible, even for a computer.

Luke: It's not impossible. I used to bull's-eye womp rats in my T-16 back home. They're not much bigger than two meters.

—from *Star Wars, Episode IV: A New Hope*

When I was twelve years old, my sister was fifteen and loved all things girly. During the preceding three or four years, doll houses and horses had given way to coordinating accessories and *Seventeen* magazine (which, to my prepubescent amazement, managed every month to come up with a new and yet more hilarious list of kissing techniques, guide to dating dos and don'ts, or manual for knowing if he *really* likes you). She loved Kirk Cameron and *St. Elmo's Fire* and all the gritty power ballads by Chicago and Air Supply.

(Want to hear a funny side story? Kirk Cameron came to speak at New Life last year, and I hosted him. In his born-again life, he is of course the star of the *Left Behind* movies and a recent voice for the revival of interpersonal-confrontation evangelism. I was getting him wired up before the service, and he commented on the high number of young men on our staff. I responded by telling him that all of us New Life pastors who grew up in the eighties felt both excited and a little awkward to have him with us. Excited because seeing him and thinking about *Growing Pains* for the first time in thirteen years was like a little slice of our childhood, and awkward because all of our wives once had a crush on him. He said something like, "Well, praise God, brother." I don't think he thought it was funny.)

Above all else, though, my sister loved Ralph Macchio. Honestly, my first inclination is to poke innocent fun at Ralph Macchio for a nice, light-hearted opening to this chapter. But now that I think about it, many of us painfully average guys in high school owed our dating lives to him. He was the poor, skinny, uncool new kid who improved himself and won the pretty girl's heart. Take away the *Seventeen*-centerfold face, and he was every kid. The *Karate Kid* had the double benefit of telling all of us non-Johnnys that we could make ourselves more appealing as well as telling the pretty girls that they shouldn't walk past ordinary guys. It made going out with the plain, skinny kid cool. Thank God.

Wax On...Wax Off

Remember in *The Karate Kid* how Daniel got beaten up by the cool California-beach-kid/black-belt crowd and then decided he needed to learn karate? How fortuitous that right around that time he met the wise and Asian-combat-savvy Mr. Miyagi. Eager to learn how to defend his skinny behind and win the girl of his dreams, Daniel showed up ready for his lesson and, to his chagrin, was put to work. "You want me to do what? Wax your antique car collection? What the junk is that?!" Determined to earn Miyagi's favor, though, Daniel gave in and waxed. He came back next time, figuring he had passed the test and would now begin learning Miyagi's aged craft; instead, it was more of the same. Paint the house. Paint the fence. On and on it went. Daniel grew more and more frustrated until he finally went off on the little man and Miyagi yelled back at him, "Wax on!" as he threw a karate punch that Daniel's wax-application action perfectly deflected. It was then Daniel realized that all the work he'd been doing that had seemed so bizarre and irrelevant was actually training.

The Sheep, the Harp, and the Armor

It wasn't so different for young David. As we've imagined, the shock would have been great, the disappointment even greater, when, after Samuel took his anointing oil and left David's home, nothing happened. For lack of any further divine encounter, heavenly conveyance, or burning-bush revelation, David was relegated once more to shepherding. So there he was, the day after being anointed, back out in the field with the sheep.

Resisting with every shred of will the impulse to manhandle the plans, David purposed instead to tend his father's sheep, write worship songs, and fend off marauding beasts. In all likelihood he did these things largely in spite of himself. Perhaps he did them because they were the right things to do or because they were all he knew to do in that moment or maybe just because he knew they needed doing, never supposing that while he helped his dad, wrote music, and fought bears, he was training for his mission. Wax on…wax off.

But how strategic were those days and months with the sheep. As we have already seen, David learned God's authority by returning home to help in the fields. David also learned God's friendship out in the field. (We'll discuss this more in depth in a later chapter.) And as became evident during Israel's Goliath crisis, David learned to fight out in the fields. First Samuel 17 depicts the Israelite army's perilous standoff with the Philistine hero:

> A champion named Goliath, who was from Gath, came out of the Philistine camp. He was over nine feet tall. He had a bronze helmet on his head and wore a coat of scale armor of bronze weighing five thousand shekels; on his legs he wore bronze greaves, and a bronze javelin was slung on his back. His spear shaft was like a weaver's rod, and its iron point weighed six hundred shekels. His shield bearer went ahead of him.
>
> Goliath stood and shouted to the ranks of Israel, "Why do you come out and line up for battle? Am I not a Philistine, and are you not the servants of Saul? Choose a man and have him come down to me. If he is able to fight and kill me, we will become your subjects; but if I overcome him and kill him, you will become our subjects and serve us."[1]

Lions and Bears Are Training Aids

Paralyzed with fear, Saul and his army hemmed and hawed as, day after day, the giant defied them to produce just one man who would fight him. Not even involved in the battle, David heard of the challenge and offered to take on Goliath. Why was David so confident when his countrymen were so mousy? He knew God, yes, but he also knew how to fight:

> David said to Saul, "Let no one lose heart on account of this Philistine; your servant will go and fight him."
>
> Saul replied, "You are not able to go out against this Philistine and fight him; you are only a boy, and he has been a fighting man from his youth."
>
> But David said to Saul, "Your servant has been keeping his father's sheep. When a lion or a bear came and carried off a sheep from the flock, I went after it, struck it and rescued the sheep from its mouth. When it turned on me, I seized it by its hair, struck it and killed it. Your servant has killed both the lion and the bear; this uncircumcised Philistine will be like one of them, because he has defied the armies of the living God. The LORD who delivered me from the paw of the lion and the paw of the bear will deliver me from the hand of this Philistine."
>
> Saul said to David, "Go, and the LORD be with you."[2]

You know the outcome:

> As the Philistine moved closer to attack him, David ran quickly toward the battle line to meet him. Reaching into his bag and

> taking out a stone, he slung it and struck the Philistine on the forehead. The stone sank into his forehead, and he fell facedown on the ground.
>
> So David triumphed over the Philistine with a sling and a stone; without a sword in his hand he struck down the Philistine and killed him.[3]

David found an opportunity to get on the royal radar screen, but it required courage and skill with a weapon. He moved into the world of kings that day—and won himself a permanent place in the hearts of the people he would one day lead—because he had killed his lions and bears. He did the work along the way, and it paid off.

Demons Apparently Don't Care for Harp Music

Another pursuit David undertook while he waited those tortuous days in the fields was playing the harp. He wrote some really good songs that became the bulk of the Bible's longest book, but he also got good at harp playing. Fortunate indeed, as it turned out, because during that time, Saul started having demon problems:

> Now the Spirit of the LORD had departed from Saul, and an evil spirit from the LORD tormented him.
>
> Saul's attendants said to him, "See, an evil spirit from God is tormenting you. Let our lord command his servants here to search for someone who can play the harp. He will play when the evil spirit from God comes upon you, and you will feel better."
>
> So Saul said to his attendants, "Find someone who plays well and bring him to me."[4]

The king's own staff, in their vast wisdom, concluded that the best way to help their boss was to ferret out the best harpist in the land and have him play during the demon attacks. This, they hypothesized, would make Saul feel better. Bizarre. But the king agreed, and totally clueless that God had earmarked the young shepherd to succeed the king, Saul's attendants sent for David. Good thing David was applying himself to the work he found along the way! His decision to cultivate his abilities while he waited gave him entrée into the world of the embattled king. What may have seemed ancillary to David proved essential to living into his calling. Wax on…wax off.

What Is and Is Not Mundane About Carrying Armor

It wasn't long before Saul grew fond of David, what with his command of the harp and its apparent soothing qualities during these tense times. As we saw in the previous chapter,

> David came to Saul and entered his service. Saul liked him very much, and David became one of his armor-bearers. Then Saul sent word to Jesse, saying, "Allow David to remain in my service, for I am pleased with him."[5]

One can imagine David's mixed feelings. On the one hand, he was now working for the king. This was decidedly closer to his future—the elusive calling of God that had come to define him on the inside—than he had ever come while out in the fields with the sheep. He was in the company of royalty now, and he was finally getting to do some more manly things than just play the harp. On the other hand, he was expecting to be the king himself, so maintaining the king's battle gear had to be sort of a letdown. At each step along the path, David must have been thinking, *Aha! This is it! Now I'm on the way to the throne. Good-bye sheep! Hello kingdom!*

So David stayed steady, took care of the armor, and took care of the king. And the good thing about being an armor bearer, as it turned out, is you learn a lot about armor, armament, arms, and the like. When David was just a demon-soothing musician, he probably kept company with the other musicians and personal attendants of the king and his family. When he became armor bearer, though, David's company suddenly changed. Rather than having discussions with the other musicians about what key to write the next march in, David was thrust into a world of discussions about where to march, and when, and with what forces. As the king's armor bearer, David found himself in battle briefings, training maneuvers, and strategy sessions. As armor bearer, he got the opportunity to learn warfare, an essential skill for a head of state and one for which most kings would have been trained from the earliest age. David's childhood had trained him to kill lions and bears—and he gained the courage and cunning that comes from such exploits—but he never learned organized warfare. To have any hope of succeeding as king, he needed to know how to plan an offensive, mobilize an army, lead troops into battle, and lay siege to a city. Good thing for his calling that he stayed the course and shined the armor. Wax on...wax off.

The Killing Business

I graduated from college knowing that (1) I was called by God to serve him, apparently in some occupational capacity; and (2) I was obligated to spend four years in the U.S. Army in return for my taxpayer-funded education. I'm pretty sure I was aware of this grim paradox during my university years, but somehow I managed to put off facing it in favor of the carefree undergraduate life. Whatever the reason, at age twenty-two I found myself slapped in the face with the shocking reality that God had unmistakably called me to the saving business, and I was working in the killing business instead.

For a while I mourned the death of my calling. I ached when I read that God had relegated the temple work to David's son because the great king had too much blood on his hands—and here I was training soldiers to go to war. Tortured thoughts raced through my mind: *What have I done? How did I not see this problem coming and get out of it somehow?* By the end of my first year of commanding a tank platoon, I was sure I had missed God's plan for my life. With every "kill" on the laser-simulated battlefield, I imagined my assignment from heaven charred and burning like so many destroyed enemy combat vehicles. I never saw actual combat, it is true, but how much simulated blood was on my hands! Other men of the cloth were beating their swords into plowshares. Not only had I not beaten my sword into any useful implement for the betterment of humankind, I had lived by it, spent the most vibrant years of my life sharpening it, and spent weeks on end in the dusty and desolate Mojave Desert honing my skills in its use.

The good news is that the brokenheartedness of feeling I'd forsaken my supposed calling never drove me away from my faith. No, I was praying, studying the Bible, serving in the church, and sharing my hope in Christ more fervently than ever. Looking back on those years, I clearly see that I was doing all the things a person ought to do when called by God to pastor people. By any account, God's blessing, protection, and favor were increasingly being poured out in my life, but I didn't see it. Everything I did—seek God, search the Scriptures, serve people—I did in spite of my certainty that, with every simulated combat operation, I was charging farther away from my calling.

Then one day it hit me. Just at the point when I was at the end of my rope and the calling appeared irretrievable, I had a Mr. Miyagi moment when he yelled "Aaaayyy!" and came at me with all his fifty-year-old bonsai-tree-grooming fury and tried to punch me and kick me, and I realized all at once that if I just painted the fence and waxed the car I could fend off his onslaught, even though he's a martial-arts master. And then I settled into the weird, humbling awareness that I had started to learn karate. Let me explain.

Our tank battalion was spending July at the National Training Center in Southern California. (If you've never spent a month in the Mojave Desert during the summer, wearing an insulated, flame-retardant suit in the tiny turret of a big metal vehicle and going without a shower the entire time, you really should try it.) Every day for several days, we fought multiple battles, and I issued operation orders to my platoon of soldiers before each one. The particular challenge of telling seasoned soldiers—many of whom were significantly older and most of whom had more experience than I—what they needed to do in such a way that I came across as credible but not condescending, humble but not clueless, was never once lost on me. I had long since gotten over the awkwardness of knowing that these men knew I was young and new in the military. I had long since resolved that I would not be intimidated, but instead would stand up straight, put my shoulders back, and lead. Still, I had never seen all of this as preparation for the calling I cherished.

But after this one operation order before this one battle in this one desert exercise on this one insufferably hot summer day, it clicked. I was on my way back to my tank from the command post in the center of our assembly area. I had just given another insipid order for another unmemorable battle, when it suddenly occurred to me that all this time I had not been going in the 180-degree opposite direction of God's calling after all. Everything I had been doing was training. The intense physical discipline was like sanding Mr. Miyagi's deck. The fish-out-of-water feeling was my "paint the fence." The frustratingly rigid insistence on submission to authority, my "wax the car." The hundreds of prosaic plans I had written and delivered, always trying to figure out how to connect with my men and make sure they really comprehended without feeling like I was patronizing them or wagging my finger—all of this was training for one vital thing: learning how to preach.

As If I'd Been Doing It My Entire Life...

I'll never forget the first time I preached. The whole day was amazing for me, but two things in particular made it remarkable. First, it was the very first time I had ever preached—ever—to anyone at all, and it happened in front of three thousand people in a jam-packed auditorium on a Sunday morning at New Life Church. Now, I have to admit that I'm still not totally sure *why* I was preaching that day, but on Friday afternoon (of two-days-before-Sunday fame), Pastor Ted called me and asked nonchalantly, unforgettably, "How'd you like to take the service Sunday morning?" Now understand, my mind went into rapid computation mode, searching for any possible sensible meaning behind my boss's question. *"Take the service." What is he talking about? Take pictures of the service? Take up the offering during the service? What on earth does he mean?* I didn't have any grid for what he had in mind. In the same instant I was trying and rejecting several dozen possible interpretations, Pastor Ted added, "Preach. Do you want to preach?" *Preach? On Sunday morning? To the whole church? Are you kidding me? I don't know how to preach! I wouldn't even know where to begin.* Then my mouth interrupted a perfectly sensible thought process: "Absolutely!"

So that Saturday night I checked myself into the World Prayer Center on our church campus (if ever there was a time I needed prayer from the whole world, it was then) and cried out to God for mercy. In the morning, I put on the one suit I owned, selected the Bible my parents had given me on confirmation day, and headed for the megachurch I had been attending for several years and serving as a staff member for a few months to preach the first sermon of my life. I was twenty-six years old.

The whole morning was surreal. I vaguely remember the well wishes of fellow staff members barely masking their nervousness for me. As I took the platform, I remember my wife sitting there all pretty and hopeful on the front row, her youthful face radiating that she believed in me the way I wanted to believe in myself. I remember thinking that if ever I'd see a breach in Pastor Ted's trademark confident nonchalance, it would be today. I remember surprised congregants greeting me afterward, thanking me for the message and asking, "Now, are you one of the interns?" I remember during the worship time believing in God like never before in my life. But most clearly and vividly of all—and this is the second amazing thing—I remember this: I was never nervous.

An inexplicable combination of heightened confidence and heightened humility came over me that morning, and by the power and grace of God, I stood up and preached as if I had been doing it my entire life. It was like a dream, really. Have you ever dreamed that you're in the NBA Championship, game seven, score tied, end of the fourth quarter, and the ball comes to you? In the dream you're not nervous at all because you're used to the pressure and you expect to get the ball, because in the dream *you're good.* Preaching for the first time was like that. It was the closest thing to an out-of-body experience I've ever had—as if I were sitting there watching myself and it was totally natural that I was preaching to three thousand adults. I'll never forget finishing and sitting down and thinking, *What just happened? How did I do that?* For a few moments I sat still, stunned and in wonder, and then I sensed the unmistakable voice of the Holy Spirit answer me, "You killed your lions and bears."

Preaching was natural because, even though I was brand new, I had practiced many, many times. I had this otherworldly feeling that I had done it before because, in truth, I had. Crafting an outline; keeping people's attention; making the message connect with them; articulating clearly; communicating humility; communicating authority. I had done it all, so very many times, and this was just one more. I had done the work along the way, sometimes in spite of myself, and now it all started fitting together. Wax on...wax off.

■ ■ ■

I talk to young adults all the time, and one of the most common attitudes I encounter in even the godliest of them is this inclination to get on to "the good stuff." The real work. Many of us desire to be done with the pettiness of whatever we're doing now so that God can start using us in powerful ways. This mind-set seems noble at first, but the insidious underbelly of pride ends up poisoning and immobilizing us. It's pride because, by despising whatever we're doing now, by considering it beneath us, too often we are rejecting the very process God has designed to prepare us for taking the next steps in our calling.

So we must never scorn or discount what our hands have found to do. If you are walking with God and surrendering your life to his service, whatever you are doing right now is useful to him. Maybe he planned it, and maybe he didn't. Either way, he can work with it to make you a person after his own heart. Maybe you're in the middle of God's perfect will, and maybe you're at the tail end of a horrendously unproductive detour. No matter, he can cause even the biggest detour to work together for your good and for the good of his kingdom. So stop thinking that flipping burgers is beneath your dignity. Quit whining about waiting tables or framing houses or working retail in the mall. It's all training, if you'll let it be. God is the one who thought of the calling you so vigilantly guard, and he is more than capable of accomplishing it through the circumstances of your life right now. You are not biding time, you are not spinning your wheels, and you are not heading the wrong direction, if only you'll allow God to turn your burgers and I-beams into lions and bears.

You Better Find Somebody to Serve

> The best way to find yourself is to lose yourself in the service of others.
>
> —Mahatma Gandhi

I was a member of New Life Church for four years prior to joining the staff. On two occasions during that season of life, I sensed the Lord speaking clearly to me. Interestingly, both occurred during a Sunday-morning service while Pastor Ted was preaching.

The first time, I was twenty-four years old, and I was serving as a tank platoon leader at the army base here in Colorado Springs. So there I sat that Sunday morning, somewhere in the middle of a sea of chairs (New Life is a church of eleven thousand), listening to the morning's message, clueless to the cosmic intersection that was about to take place. Just like before—on the desert plains of Africa and in the tank commander's turret in the wee hours of the morning—I sensed with absolute certainty that, for some reason eternally unknowable to me, the God of Abraham, Isaac, and Jacob had chosen that random moment to give me the next piece of the puzzle. And here's what happened: As I sat there listening, the room seemed to fall silent, but Pastor Ted kept moving around the platform. Then he turned toward me, and it was as though he were speaking directly to me. Next he "chopped" right at me (Pastor Ted frequently chops when he preaches—it's a favorite hand gesture for driving a point home), and I sensed the Lord say, *You will serve him someday.*

Now understand that, at this point, I had never met Pastor Ted. Of course, I knew him from sitting in church and listening to him week after week, but he didn't know me from a Chinese acrobat. We later became acquainted when I volunteered in the high-school ministry and he officiated at my wedding, but at this point I was just a face in the crowd. From a purely statistical standpoint, my engineer's brain was quick to point out that the odds of my premonition coming to pass were astronomical. But by this time, I possessed a sort of serene certainty about God's revelations concerning my life. Like the boy Samuel, I found myself more clued in the third time around. I adopted the tack of Mary, the mother of Jesus, whose response to the shocking angelic revelation was to treasure these things and ponder them in her heart.

About a year later, sitting in the same area of that sea of chairs during another Suday-morning service, it happened again. Same format, different message. This time: *You are going to preach from this platform.*

Now I'm going to tell you how these two premonitions came to pass. Skip over two more years of wearing camouflage suits to work every day, of preparing battle orders for tank-battalion attacks, and, finally, of working a desk job on the commanding general's staff. By the time I was in the fourth year of my four-year service obligation, I was no longer going out to the field for weeks on end without a shower and eating prepackaged meals with disturbingly long shelf lives. Instead, I was working in an air-conditioned office in front of a computer most of the day, preparing lengthy PowerPoint briefings for colonels to give to generals about the status of our installation and the combat readiness of the units headquartered there. And the weirdest part about this stage of my army career—which really bears very little on the point of the book but is nonetheless amusing—is that I worked with four middle-aged women. One lieutenant colonel, one senior noncommissioned officer, two Department of the Army civilians, all of them committed to the national defense in the employ of the U.S. taxpayer. And me, a twenty-five-year-old, looking forward to my next career.

Atypical though it was, this season taught me invaluable lessons about how to work with, remain composed around, anticipate the needs of, accommodate the whims of—in other words, how to serve—executive-level leaders. (Remember chapter 6? Do the work along the way, with your attitude straight, as if it's what you're going to do for the rest of your life. Everything is training.)

Well, I was sitting at my desk one day, working on slide 127, when Pastor Ted called. He was so natural. I was shocked. We were acquainted by now, but I was not accustomed to receiving calls from him at work. He asked me when I would be getting out of the army, and I told him I had four more months. Then he asked if I would pray about coming to work for him when I got out. My response was something like this: "Let me pray about that... Yes!"

I didn't need to pray about it. I didn't even need to think about it, because I had been praying and thinking about it for the past three years. I knew. Wanting not to be impetuous, though, I went up to the mountains the following weekend to pray and fast about this new direction. There I read something in the Bible that jumped off the page and wrapped itself around my heart.

The One Who Used to Pour Water...

First Kings 19 tells about the lowest point in the prophet Elijah's life. Fearful of Jezebel's death threat, he journeyed alone into the desert, "came to a broom tree, sat down under it and prayed that he might die. 'I have had enough, LORD,' he said. 'Take my life; I am no better than my ancestors.' "[1]

A little later, "the word of the LORD came to him: 'What are you doing here, Elijah?' He replied, 'I have been very zealous for the LORD God Almighty. The Israelites have rejected your covenant, broken down your altars, and put your prophets to death with the sword. I am the only one left, and now they are trying to kill me too.' "[2]

It was during this season of Elijah's life that Elisha entered the scene. On his way home from the encounter with God, Elijah "found Elisha son of Shaphat...plowing with twelve yoke of oxen, and he himself was driving the twelfth pair. Elijah went up to him and threw his cloak around him.... [Elisha] took his yoke of oxen and slaughtered them. He burned the plowing equipment to cook the meat and gave it to the people, and they ate. Then he set out to follow Elijah and *became his attendant.*"[3]

Elisha, the man most people think of as a great prophet, worker of miracles, inheritor of the double portion of Elijah's power, was actually called to be Elijah's attendant. His attaché. His servant. It's easy to think that all the servant talk was a mere formality, that Elisha knew who he was really going to be. Becoming Elijah's attendant was probably just a rite of passage. Surely, both men knew the real deal. Or maybe Elisha was doing the self-deprecation thing, trying to be humble and not gloat over his planned rise to power and prominence. Whatever the reason, the servant talk was just lip service, right?

Look at this. Not long after Elijah had gone up to heaven in the flaming chariot, the kings of Israel and Judah joined forces in battle:

> King Joram set out from Samaria and mobilized all Israel. He also sent this message to Jehoshaphat king of Judah: "The king of Moab has rebelled against me. Will you go with me to fight against Moab?"
>
> "I will go with you," he replied. "I am as you are, my people as your people, my horses as your horses."[4]

The armies set out together, and it wasn't long before they were in a pinch. The king of Judah (good king) asked the king of Israel (bad king), "Is there no prophet of the LORD here, that we may inquire of the LORD through him?"[5] The wicked king of Israel might have been able to point the way to a liquor store or a house of ill repute, but he was clueless about anything to do with God. An officer of the king chimed in, though, and what an interesting insight we gain from his comment: "Elisha son of Shaphat is here. He used to pour water on the hands of Elijah."[6]

Notice that at this juncture—even after Elijah had been taken up to heaven—Elisha was known only as the one who used to pour water on the hands of Elijah. You would think that if Elisha had been groomed as the heir apparent to Elijah Ministries, that fact would already have been known. It seems instead that Elisha was known only for what he had been all those intervening years: Elijah's servant.

And that is what the Lord revealed to me as I asked him about going to work for New Life Church: *You are to be the man who pours water on the hands of Ted Haggard.*

And that is what I have had the privilege of doing all these years. Serving Pastor Ted. Now I lead one of New Life's weekend services, but that is not the main thing God has called me to do. I preach on Saturday nights because Pastor Ted asked me to. Insofar as it serves him to do it, I preach and lead with all my heart. But I would consider it every bit as much my calling to pick up his laundry, organize his desk, answer his phone, or mow his lawn. God has not explicitly assigned me to pastor a postmodern congregation within New Life Church, though to the extent that it serves Pastor Ted, you could say I do. God has not instructed me to sit at Starbucks and talk with young men, but because it advances God's purposes for Pastor Ted, I do it almost every day.

Don't Confuse the Dream and the Calling

It's important to note here that when I say that God has not instructed me to preach or to lead his people in my generation, I'm not saying that I haven't *wanted* to do these things. I have all kinds of dreams. My heart bursts with them. I've observed over the years that a variety of things seem to motivate people, from wealth to fame to power to happiness. None of these has ever motivated me. What does motivate me—what keeps me awake at night staring at the ceiling with the wheels turning in my mind as I try to lie still and not wake up my wife—is mattering in people's lives.

Ever since I was a boy, I've wanted to make a difference. In junior high I joined Greenpeace because I wanted to help save the earth from the unrelenting increase in global temperature, the subsequent melting of the polar ice caps, and the imminent cataclysm that it all spelled. In high school I joined the Sierra Club because I wanted to help rescue the dolphins that were getting caught in tuna nets. In college I joined Amnesty International because I wanted to help defend the people whose basic human rights were being trampled. (Shortly after this time I figured out that all the groups I'd been joining for years are actually hyperliberal political-action organizations. I was disappointed and a little embarrassed that my decade of fifteen-dollar contributions had really gone toward the vain attempt to get Michael Dukakis elected president.) Then I gave my life to Christ, and ever since that time my heart has burned for the purposes of God for my generation of believers.

God confirmed on that desert plain in Africa that he was the author of my dreams of mattering. But instead of giving me specific instructions, he intimated only that I would serve him for the rest of my life—and love it. That's pretty broad. So I had dreams—big, grandiose, off-the-wall dreams—and I had a sense of calling to vocational ministry, and until the day in church when I witnessed the sudden silence and Pastor Ted's hand chop, and then the ratification three years later when I received the shocking phone call while preparing a PowerPoint presentation, that was all I had.

Never confuse the dream and the calling. The idea is to live the calling—obey in full at every point along the path—and grow into the dream. You mustn't get restless when the calling isn't as exciting as the dream.

A King Serving a King

As we've already seen, Saul started having demon problems sometime after God had rejected him as king and chosen David to succeed him. But notice this story from a different angle: David was there in the fields, watching the sheep, dreaming about being king. His thoughts on those excruciatingly normal days must have wandered to heroic campaigns, multination treaties, and beautiful queens. Many dreams he must have dreamed; many grand designs he surely imagined that would flesh out his calling. His dreams were the stuff of fables.

Then came the next piece of the puzzle—David's PowerPoint phone call:

> Saul sent messengers to Jesse and said, "Send me your son David, who is with the sheep." So Jesse took a donkey loaded with bread, a skin of wine and a young goat and sent them with his son David to Saul.
>
> David came to Saul and *entered his service.*[7]

It's easy to look at this turn in the plot as one step closer to kingship for David—and indeed it was that. But also consider this development for what it is: David's dream was to be king, and instead he became a servant. His calling as it stood at that time was to do what Saul wanted done—to take care of Saul's armor and play the harp. These things were a far cry from the fabulous dreams of the pasture. These were not the tasks kings did. Kings didn't serve kings.

Here is another indispensable lesson from David's path to power: He didn't despise or begrudge servanthood; he embraced it. When Saul's life was defined by the pressure from the Philistines, relieving that pressure became David's cause. In response to the taunts of the warrior Goliath, "David said to Saul, 'Let no one lose heart on account of this Philistine...'" And the younger man's heart shone through as he humbled himself and offered himself for the sake of his king: "'Your servant will go and fight him.'"[8]

I don't suppose David stopped dreaming of being king during those years. How could he forget Samuel's visit? No, those dreams stayed with him. They burned in him, haunted him, preoccupied him at times. He didn't pretend that God hadn't anointed him, he didn't try to give himself some kind of positive-thinking mind job, and he didn't sulk because being the king's servant wasn't what he was made to do. David knew exactly what he was getting into, and he plunged into servanthood head first.

The Fundamental Theorem of Jesus

As I've taught the Bible over the years, it has occurred to me that most of Jesus's teachings boil down to a handful of core truths. One of these is the paradoxical relationship between our calling and our dreams. I call it the Fundamental Theorem of Jesus because no idea for good living is more central to Jesus's message than this one. In Matthew 16:24-25,

> Jesus said to his disciples, "If anyone would come after me, he must deny himself and take up his cross and follow me. For whoever wants to save his life will lose it, but whoever loses his life for me will find it."

Jesus seemed to acknowledge that we all have dreams, but when we try to make them happen ourselves—when we ramrod them through in an attempt to save our lives—they slip right through our fingers. But when we subordinate them, lay them aside—die to our heart's dreams and lose our lives for Christ—then our dreams advance. In response to the disciples' discussion of their dreams of greatness, Jesus punctuated this idea of laying down our lives and dreams, saying, "Whoever wants to become great among you must be your servant."[9]

Somehow, intuitively, David knew this. Centuries before Christ was even born, David was losing his life in order to find it. Having greater certainty about his dreams than most, he still chose to serve; he even embraced subservience. He must have figured out that there is some cosmic relationship, some value-connect of God's, between serving someone and finding your life in abundance. David learned this great truth: If you want to see your dreams fulfilled, you better find somebody to serve. And how it paid off for him!

Flag Boy

When I started working at New Life, I had no idea what I would do on a day-to-day basis. This much was clear: God had called me to serve Pastor Ted, and now Pastor Ted had called and asked me to do the same thing. So I would serve Pastor Ted, and that's about all I knew. In fact, I remember saying to him something like, "I'm so excited to start working for you at New Life, and I'm so grateful for the opportunity to serve you. So…I was wondering…what exactly will I be…um…*doing* for you?"

His response was unforgettable: "Oh, I have no idea. I just like you."

Indeed, my job was (and is) to do what Pastor Ted needs doing. The first Sunday morning of my employ with New Life found me on the front row where all the pastors sit. I was adorned in the one suit I owned, brimming with the expectation of a man who has been called and wondering what on earth I would be doing. During the worship time, Pastor Ted approached me with a smile, welcomed me to the team, and said, "See the flags hanging from the ceiling?" (In our old auditorium, the flags of all the nations of the 10/40 Window hung from the rafters as a reminder to pray for the people of these spiritually dark countries.)

"Um...yes," I replied.

"Well, I've been thinking about rearranging those flags to reflect both the 10/40 and 40/70 Windows. What do you think about that?" (The 10/40 and 40/70 prayer campaigns target the regions of the earth that fall within areas or windows that extend from 10 to 40 degrees and 40 to 70 degrees north latitude, respectively. These are the regions of the world where the vast majority of the remaining unreached people groups reside. It is the spiritually darkest part of the globe and the most strategic target for our prayers, resources, and missionaries.)

"Uh..." *How random! What else is there to say here?* "Sounds great."

"All right. Well, how would you like to take point on that project?"

There's only one right answer to that: "I'd love to."

So there it was. My first job was to rearrange the flags that hung from the ceiling of our main auditorium. Now, you have to get the picture: I'm not talking about just a couple of flags. There were dozens, scores, probably hundreds of flags. And they were painstakingly arranged in alphabetical order, all precisely the same height and with staggering symmetry. I thought about the type of person who must have hung those flags. My imagination ran wild—what amazing precision, what a dizzying sense of compliance must have gripped him all the time! His gift for precision could have known no bounds. My musings were confirmed Monday morning when I put on an old pair of blue jeans and a T-shirt, raised myself up to the rafters on a Genie Lift, and inspected the rigging apparatus that had been devised to hang and level the flags. It was shockingly complex. An intricate system of PVC pipe, custom fabricated sheet metal, fishing line, lead weights, and rare Southeast Asian fisherman's knots kept each flag aloft and perfectly in line with all the others.

For the next several weeks, I systematically took down and rehung the flags. You'd think it would have been a pretty straightforward operation, but it turned out to be quite involved. Before removing a row of flags, I had to clear a wide enough swath amid the auditorium chairs to navigate the Genie Lift safely beneath the flags. This was stupidly tricky because I didn't know exactly where I needed the lift to be until I was up in the air much nearer the flags. So up I'd go and then realize I needed to be five feet to the left. Then I'd go back down, move more chairs, go back up, repeat the process all day, then move all the chairs back to their original positions in time for the youth meeting that night—and do it all again the next day.

I also had to determine just which countries were and were not in each Window, find the flags for those nations that we didn't already possess, fabricate new sheet-metal country ID signs to match the existing ones, get a blueprint of the rafters from the architect, plan where all two Windows' worth of flags would go, try to replicate my predecessor's byzantine system of suspension, fail, create a new (and, I must say, much simpler) system of suspending the flags from the rafters, move and put back the auditorium chairs several dozen times, endure the maddening suggestions of my superiors as to the many reasons the flags ought to be arranged or oriented differently from how I had painstakingly placed them, remove the flag of the tiny, frail nation that had ceased to exist while I was up in the rafters (it was a lot like the Tom Hanks movie *The Terminal,* in which his country went away while he was in an airplane—

both intriguing and highly inconvenient), move all subsequent flags down one space, and have it all done in time for our rapidly approaching annual pastors conference. And I did it all alone. It was memorable.

What I Learned on the Genie Lift

That month I found myself in a situation that was new to me: For hours upon hours I was twenty-five feet in the air on a Genie Lift, alone, doing something with which I was not enthralled. And I found myself wrestling with some of life's most important thoughts during those hours on the lift.

For the first week, I was just excited to be on staff at New Life Church.

By the second week, I was thinking a lot about the Wall Street investment-banking career I had turned down to come work at New Life.

Come week three, I was all fired up inside: *This is not what I'm called to do! Look at me, up here in the rafters in old blue jeans, breathing dust every day. Look at me—I'm Flag Boy! This is not what I signed up for!*

It was during week four that it hit me. (Some people only require a few days or a week in the rafters, but I needed a month to figure it out.) This *is* what I am called to do. God had shown me only this: that I was to serve Ted Haggard. And serving Ted meant doing what Ted wanted done. It was my calling—to serve Ted—and in a way, it was my salvation. Because over the past few years of doing all that I could possibly do to get done what Ted wanted done, I lived into all the parts of my calling that I had desired.

You want to live into the dreams God has placed in your heart? You better find somebody to serve. You want to do the things you want to do? It's time to start accomplishing what God has put in someone else's heart. You have to lose it if you want to find it.

Chapter 9

You Gotta Lose It to Find it

How come everybody wanna keep it like the kaiser?
Give it away give it away give it away now.
—Red Hot Chili Peppers

So I knew this: I was going to serve God for the rest of my life, and I was going to love it; I was to serve Ted Haggard; and one day I was to preach from the platform of the church I loved so dearly. At the age of twenty-six, I was "serving God" in the vocational sense that I had taken the Princess Leia-esque download to mean all those years ago. And I was serving Ted. But what about the rest? *What about the good stuff? When do I pastor? When do I preach? Come on, God, I know there's more!*

My season of flags was followed by a season that was—to my Presbyterian sensibilities anyway—confusing and strange, and then by another that was heartbreaking. By the time I came down from the rafters a month after I had begun, it had been determined that the best place for me to plug in and help was at the World Prayer Center. The center is a unique bluish building on New Life Church's campus that looks like the starship *Enterprise.* It was conceived during the AD2000 Movement in the 1990s for the purpose of coordinating global prayer toward the completion of the Great Commission. It had recently been completed—the building, not the Great Commission—and was in the final stages of being staffed and chartered to encourage prayer in our community and around the world. I was to be assistant to the director.

The World Prayer Center functioned like a department of New Life Church, and its director and other staff were New Life employees, but it developed a distinct culture from that of the church. I went into that assignment armed with my newly gained prayer-window knowledge (I now knew more about the history, composition, and strategic significance of the 10/40 and 40/70 Window nation flags than anyone I knew) and was excited to help. I was met with some fun surprises.

In retrospect, plunging my Presbyterian self into the culture of the World Prayer Center was not unlike Alice plunging down the rabbit hole. I had entered a sort of spiritual Wonderland where everything was kind of familiar but ceaselessly interesting and totally bizarre. In keeping with his philosophy of delegating authority, Pastor Ted had empowered others with the leadership of some of the prayer meetings at the Prayer Center. Consequently, there was a colorful array of people involved. For example, I watched this scene stealthily for about a month before figuring out what was going on: Every morning at precisely eight o'clock, a kind-looking older gentleman would go to the atrium in the middle of the building, stand facing what I deduced after a couple weeks of watching to be the four cardinal directions, and blow into a long, painful sounding, and awful smelling animal horn. The sound it made was something like a cross between Braveheart's battle cry and dying cattle. (Of course, I later learned that this instrument was a *shofar* and that it is a fixture in many charismatic church cultures. I never learned, however, (1) why, although this animal part was the best they had to work with in the Old Testament era, it isn't considered as spiritually potent today to avail ourselves of five thousand years of music technology and play, say, a trumpet; or (2) why, when we can monitor the heart rhythms of an astronaut in the earth's orbit from an office in coastal Texas, we cannot concoct some chemical to neutralize that horrible smell.)

Working in the World Prayer Center was a wonderful experience both of learning the world into which I was being adopted and of having the opportunity to lose my life in practical ways each day. Ever since I had sensed the Lord's calling all those years before, I had had clear, sensible ideas as to what it would all look like and how it would all unfold. Without exactly realizing it, I was wanting to *find* my life—to define it, grasp it, and make it happen—but the Fundamental Theorem of Jesus said that if you want to find it, lose it. I learned to lose my life in those years, and it was sometimes delightful and sometimes painful. That time was a systematic letting go of the mores that made me feel safe and an embracing of so much that was different. But mostly it was clinging to Jesus and confessing at the end of the day those memorable words from Peter's life-losing season: "To whom shall we go? You have the words of eternal life."[1]

Letting go of my well-laid plans and giving my life away meant ceasing to be in control, and that was, it seems now, simultaneously challenging to me and amusing to God. You have to understand, I was the black sheep of the church staff. I did not graduate from Oral Roberts University, I cannot do a funny impersonation of Rodney Howard-Browne, and I did not know that there are twenty-first-century Christians who use Hebrew prayer shawls. I was on a steep learning curve.

A Most Unexpected Path

The Oil of Gladness and the Oil of Sudden, Stinging Pain

Here's a funny story: Every weekday at noon, a worship and prayer time takes place in the chapel of the World Prayer Center, and one day I was there praying. I was sitting alone in a seat toward the back when two sweet women from the World Prayer Center staff approached me and asked if they could pray for me. They told me they sensed an anointing on my life. I took that to be a good thing and accepted their offer. They came around behind me and stood over me, and with my peripheral vision, I caught a fleeting glimpse of one of the women removing what looked like a large, green olive-oil bottle from her purse. For a split second I thought about the ominous bottle and worried about what they were going to do with it, and then before I could really put it all together,

I felt their hands grasping my head and oil being poured on my hair. Those women must have slathered me with half the bottle, because as they fervently implored God to increase his anointing on my life, the fifteen or twenty fluid ounces of olive oil that they dumped on my head started running down my forehead and down the back of my neck. It was super gross and yet strangely exciting to have olive oil cascading into my ears and inside the collar of my shirt, and then gross and exciting gave way to excruciatingly painful when the bead that had been forming on my brow fell into my eye. I don't know if you've ever had a lot of olive oil in your eyes, but it stings horribly, so I started weeping uncontrollably. Well, when the fervently praying women saw me starting to weep, they evidently felt as though their prayers were working and the anointing was falling on me because they started shouting hallelujahs and praising God, their steely grip still fixed on the crown of my head as I wept and thought, *Dear God, please make them stop!* I prayed for them to release me and imagined at the same time that this would be a great torture tactic to extract information from enemy captives.

For all I know, that could have been God anointing me. Perhaps that was my moment. The point is, none of this is what I imagined the calling to look like. This was not the trajectory I envisioned for the fulfillment of God's dreams in my heart. And even though it's easy to look back now and see how God was working it all together, it wasn't easy to see then. Now I realize that I was living the Fundamental Theorem of Jesus—losing my life in order to find it—but at the time, in the middle of the losing, it wasn't so evident because I hadn't found much yet. And therein lies the core of this secret for living into your calling: Embrace the losing season as much as you do the finding season. Maybe embrace it more because the degree to which we authentically lose determines the degree to which we authentically find.

Launch Time, or So I Thought

I've told you how I had sensed the Lord telling me I would preach from the platform of New Life Church and described the first time it happened. Now let me tell you about the events that led up to that amazing day.

I was working at the World Prayer Center and growing increasingly eager to see how the *You-will-preach-from-this-platform* part of the drama would come to pass. Mind you, I had never preached in my entire life. I was an engineer, I was a tanker, and I was a pretty good flag hanger, but I seemed to myself the furthest thing from a preacher. That's what made that part of the download so strange and wonderful and this part of the story so humbling. Here's how it happened.

I spent the better part of my first year on New Life Church staff happily assisting the director and staff of the World Prayer Center. Toward the end of that time, I had a memorable week. I was praying one morning and began to plead with God. "Launch me! You've given me the dreams of pastoring and preaching," I remember petitioning. "Now, please, please, let me do it!" There was no rending of the heavens and coming down of the heavenly host or tearing in two of the World Prayer Center curtains, but God responded in an amazing way. The first reply came while I was in the Prayer Center chapel two days later. A wise and mature woman in the church approached me. She apologized for interrupting me, introduced herself, and proceeded to tell me how God had shown her while I was praying that he was preparing to "launch" me. Those were her words. She didn't know what they meant but felt confident I would. I did.

The second response came the following weekend. A prominent worship leader was at New Life for a worship seminar, and he stayed to speak in our Sunday-evening service. As was my custom, I was pacing and praying during the song service that night when suddenly, from behind, this man's arms enveloped me and—*thunk!*—his hands landed on my chest. Surprised and feeling accosted, I turned awkwardly to see whose embrace held me captive. You can imagine my shock when I saw that it was our esteemed guest! We had not met, and he was not aware that I was part of the church staff. He apologized for interrupting me, introduced himself, and in a kind, fatherly tone explained that while I was praying, the Lord had shown him a picture. He described the scene of a space shuttle being pulled out of its hangar by a tractor, placed on the launch pad by a large crane, and then...being launched. He said God showed him that was me, that God was getting ready to launch me.

So there it was, made plain and unmistakable. Whispered in my heart and twice confirmed, in plain English. It was time. I started the next week with "Eye of the Tiger" playing in my head. I was about to get my game on. I had lost my life to the shofars, and now it was time to find it.

At this juncture came the most unexpected plot twist. That very week, totally unforeseen, our longtime youth pastor announced that it was time for him to move on. Pastor Ted told the staff that he would be choosing a new youth pastor from the inside, so anyone who wanted to be considered for the position should let him know. Well, I knew I was the man for the job. I might as well have seen Christ in a blinding light on the road to Damascus. It was that clear. And it was so right! Not only was the timing vis-à-vis the "launch" messages astronomically unlikely, but I had been serving for the past four years in the youth ministry. I led a small group of more than sixty high-school kids. I had taken cumulative weeks of my army leave time over the past several years to go to camps and retreats. I had poured my life into those kids and into serving our outgoing youth pastor. He had made me a sort of protégé. And—get this—the youth group had just that fall outgrown its meeting room and had moved into the main auditorium that was used for Sunday services, which meant that the new youth pastor would preach from the very platform from which Pastor Ted had hand-chopped when I heard the Lord so unmistakably! It was all so right it made me want to stand up and shout. At last, everything was coming together.

The pool of applicants narrowed until it was just two of us. The other candidate was an affable young staff member named Brent, who, like me, had come on board during the past year and was working in the youth department (and who has, incidentally, since become a good friend). Over the next several weeks, Brent and I were subjected to endless meetings and interviews and office pools and speculations exchanged over the coffeepot and the copier. The drama was thrilling, the suspense growing with each day that passed. I feigned the appropriate nervous uncertainty, but in my heart I knew. This was it.

When finally the decision was made, I was so sure that this was the next step in the unfolding of God's calling in my life that the phone call from Pastor Ted and the news that he had chosen Brent didn't even compute at first. The words caused a processing error in my brain that left me slack jawed and silent for an awkwardly long time. Pastor Ted finally asked, "Rob...are you there?" and I came to. Then the realization washed over me, and I felt crushed under the weight of a much larger fallen tower than just not getting the youth pastor job. This wasn't about being youth pastor, it was about my twelve-year journey of living into the dreams that God—God, not me!—had put in my heart. The tower that came crashing down was not the job; it was the very dreams God had given me.

I gradually came to recognize God's providence in the youth-pastor selection process, but at first I failed to see it. Scooping myself up off the floor took a few days. I was heartbroken. The dejection I felt dwarfed even the emotional nadir that followed my ill-fated wedding attempt. That depression had been almost artificial and removed, for I knew at the end of the day that Mauri and I would still get married. This depression bit harder because the loss was actual and final.

In all I pouted for about a week and a half, and then I got over being sad and evolved into being angry. I was angry with Pastor Ted for having toyed with the sacred God-dreams I cherished, angry with Brent for having stolen my birthright, angry with rest of the world for smiling serenely at the news of Brent's victory without even noticing the travesty that had been perpetrated against the Almighty's cosmic design. As it turned out, my anger lasted only a couple of days because I'm really not very good at staying angry with people. Soon my short-lived vehemence yielded to a sort of passive acceptance. With little emotional energy left to rue the death of my God-dream, I resigned myself to the cruel fate of missing my calling after having been so very, very close.

Launching, for Real This Time

The following week the plot took a Hitchcockian turn. It was Friday afternoon, and I was setting up my things in the cubicle outside Brent's new office. (I should add that it rapidly became clear to me and everybody else that Brent is God's man for that job. The youth group has exploded under his leadership, he is a youth preaching machine, and kids and parents adore him.) I was feeling down, but I was trying to build myself up in the Lord. Then the phone rang. It was Ted. And, well, you know the story: "Say, I was thinking, how would you like to take the first service this Sunday?"

As I've already told you, my first time ever preaching—*ever*—was in front of three thousand people on a Sunday morning at New Life Church. Indulge me as I discuss that day a bit more, because it was one of the two or three most meaningful in my life so far, and—to the point of this book—it was one of the two or three most pivotal events in the working out of my calling in Christ. That day had several remarkable aspects, but none more remarkable than the fact that, amid the emotional fog that enshrouded everything, I was never nervous. Not once. It was almost literally an out-of-body experience. I watched myself get up there, pray, open the Bible, and start teaching the people as if I had been doing it all my life. And I had no earthly idea how it was happening. It was like in *The Matrix* when Neo finished his training simulation and realized he knew jujitsu. It was completely surreal to me.

I was supposed to preach in the first service, and Pastor Ted was slated for the second. Well, I must have done reasonably well, because sometime between services, he told me I was going to speak again in the second service. I'll never forget going upstairs to the office area, locking myself in the staff bathroom, and splashing cold water on my face to clear my head and make sure I wasn't dreaming this whole thing. Then I looked at myself in the mirror and thought, *How did I do that? Can I do it again?* It's amusing in retrospect, but it was quite serious at the time. I was unclear what had happened and unsure whether I could replicate it. But I dried myself off, straightened my tie, and headed back down to the auditorium. I did do it again, and the message was well received, and I was overwhelmed. Toward the end of the sermon, there came a point when I was speaking to the people sitting in the area where I used to sit all those years ago. All at once, while I was talking, I saw that one chair, the one I used to sit in, remembered Pastor Ted's chops and the mysterious sense that God was speaking to me, and realized it had happened. It had all happened. Just when I thought I was at my lowest point, God launched me. And my life has never been the same since.

Expect to Get It Back and Be Surprised by What It Looks Like

The thing about succeeding—advancing, making it, finding your life—is that you have to lose your life willingly. We do a lot of mental gymnastics trying to fabricate this process, and they just don't work. You can't lose your life with one eye open, expecting to find it again a certain way. You can't send your life off to the dry cleaners, knowing exactly the improved condition it will be in when you get it back. It doesn't work like that. You have to lose your life. Period. Because here's the thing: You don't know what you're going to get back. You try to rig it, thinking you can work the system because you have the outcome in mind. You know what you want to get back, but that means you haven't really given anything away.

It's important to realize that this doesn't mean you shouldn't expect blessing when you give your life away. Jesus told his disciples—the ones who had left everything to follow him—"No one who has left home or brothers or sisters or mother or father or children or fields for me and the gospel will fail to receive a hundred times as much in this present age."[2] After telling them just a little bit earlier that anyone who aspired to be his follower "must deny himself and take up his cross and follow me," and adding the troubling explanation that "whoever wants to save his life will lose it, but whoever loses his life for me and for the gospel will save it,"[3] Jesus came full circle and promised that his followers would get back a better version of their lives. He assured them of blessing, and he assures you, too.

David Had Game

This is precisely what happened to David. He had his dreams. They were big and they were real, and still he chose to give his life away to serve Saul. Now, make no mistake—David was anticipating getting his life back, but he hadn't a clue when or how or in what condition, and he was okay with that. He soothed Saul's demons and cleaned Saul's armor and brought his brothers food on the battlefield. And when he had a minute, he went back home to help his dad, all the while knowing his dream. He remembered quite vividly that he was going to be king. Still, in those pivotal years of waiting and training and living into that dream, David gave his life away. He served and served and served, and he had no idea what he was going to get back.

Like me, David had his launch on a routine day. Having been at his father's house, "early in the morning David left the flock with a shepherd, loaded up and set out, as Jesse had directed."[4] He was to visit and bring rations to his brothers who were with the army of Israel, staged for battle against the Philistines. What he saw that day, though, changed his life forever:

> He reached the camp as the army was going out to its battle positions, shouting the war cry. Israel and the Philistines were drawing up their lines facing each other. David left his things with the keeper of supplies, ran to the battle lines and greeted his brothers. As he was talking with them, Goliath, the Philistine champion from Gath, stepped out from his lines and shouted his usual defiance, and David heard it. When the Israelites saw the man, they all ran from him in great fear.[5]

That scene made an indelible impression on the young man. The brazen defiance of the Philistine warrior, the embarrassing cowardice of his own people, the monumental significance of the battle that would inevitably take place—it all stacked up in David's mind like a bonfire waiting to be lighted. Just what spark ignited the conflagration we can't know for sure, but in that moment, something snapped inside him.

Before he had time to second-guess himself, David approached the king: "Let no one lose heart on account of this Philistine; your servant will go and fight him."[6]

There. He said it, before his better judgment had time to chime in.

Later that day David squared off against Goliath. Standing in the face of such overwhelming strength and hatred, with the eyes of all Israel on him, David responded as if he'd been fighting battles all his life. Just as the scene had played out hundreds of times in his childhood dreams, when the battle was on the line, David was the go-to guy, and he had game. So now he faced the giant:

> You come against me with sword and spear and javelin, but I come against you in the name of the LORD Almighty, the God of the armies of Israel, whom you have defied. This day the LORD will hand you over to me, and I'll strike you down and cut off your head. Today I will give the carcasses of the Philistine army to the birds of the air and the beasts of the earth, and the whole world will know that there is a God in Israel. All those gathered here will know that it is not by sword or spear that the LORD saves; for the battle is the LORD's, and he will give all of you into our hands.[7]

David, of course, prevailed against Goliath, and his new life began that day. From then on, the people of Israel celebrated him, and he became known for his warrior's skill and valor. He never went back to the pasture. A day that began like any other ended up being his launch day. He found his life again because he had so fully given it away.

Chapter 10

The David Doctrine

What makes resisting temptation difficult for many people is that they don't want to discourage it completely.

—Benjamin Franklin

As a kid I imagined that pastors got a special infusion of holiness. The way, I suppose, all of us once thought our parents received some kind of instruction manual or *Matrix*-esque jujitsu download of parenting knowledge. And then the day came when we had our first kid and realized that we are exactly the same people we were yesterday—no wiser, no more skilled or better prepared to raise little inept people into functional, godly humans. We are exactly the same people when we come home from the hospital as we were before we went, except that we now have a small, red screaming being to figure out how to care for.

In a similar way, I used to imagine somewhat naively that pastors received a special *Matrix*-esque jujitsu download of holiness once they made the transition from ordinary citizens to men of the cloth.

That impression was rudely shattered when I was twelve and the pastor of the church my family was attending—my pastor!—stood in the pulpit one Sunday morning and made the following announcement: "I have secretly been in love with *[insert name of deacon's wife]* for several months, so now I am leaving *[insert name of beleaguered and distraught pastor's wife]* and *[insert name of church]*, and *[insert name of deacon's wife]* and I are going to *[insert name of exotic tropical island]* together to pursue our happiness."

With the shock that comes when your entire worldview is turned upside down, I quickly realized that no holiness wand gets waved and no stop-sinning pixie dust is sprinkled over a pastor when he starts being addressed by that title. This took a while to sink into my preadolescent mind, but it finally resolved into a core conviction. Did Bruce Springsteen have the good-singer-and-guitar-player wand waved over him when he got his first record contract? Did my hero, Larry Bird, get a good-free-throw-shooting pill when he put on the Celtics jersey? Absolutely not!

They cultivated their callings, worked on them during practice, and refined their abilities long before they ever made it to stardom. My pastor didn't live a holy life as a Christian leader because he never worked out holiness as a layman.

That experience made a lasting impression on me. A decade later, having received the call from God to serve him for the rest of my life and having begun to perceive that the expression of that calling would be local church ministry, the memory of my brazenly fallen pastor frightened me. *How do I expect to do any better that he did? He was a powerful man of God, and he fell. So now I'm going to be a pastor. What chance do I have?*

After several weeks of soul searching and inner wrestling, I had little reason to believe that I would be any different at all. Let's face it: What could I do better than this mighty man of God whom we listened to with righteous fear each Sunday morning as he explained the intricate subtleties of the Bible? Come on! The pastor?! He's Mr. Holy! If this is what becomes of him, what hope have I?

Left to myself, I knew I was no better than the man I once revered as holy, and I certainly had no lingering illusion that I would somehow get holiness once I became a pastor. So there seemed to be only one viable option, and that was to *start holiness now.* To figure out how to become a man who would live out the calling of God and not buckle under the weight of sin's allure—and to start it *now,* before the stakes were high. Everyone was counting on the pastor to be holy, but who was looking at me? (Except my ever-vigilant mother, who I suspect had her doubts about any real prospect of enduring holiness in me.) I needed to start now, before the heat was turned up high. You see, people expect each of us—whatever our calling may be—to have our stuff together when we get *there,* but now, *now* is the time to dig in because not so many are watching us or even care. Now is the time to wrestle with the old sin nature, wrangle with the devil and his demons, resist the pleasures of the world that so entice us, and start cutting ourselves free of the sin that entangles. To live into our calling, we need to start holiness now.

So how do we start holiness now? What practical steps can we take to insulate ourselves from the disaster I saw in church as a child? This question is the subject of the next two chapters. Before tackling this topic, though, let me raise a more foundational question, the answer to which will color your thinking on holiness.

Can I Stop Sinning?

As we consider the prospect of starting holiness now, it begs the question of what happens *then?* At some point in the journey, will we reach our goal? This question fascinates me, as it has fascinated Bible scholars for centuries. It seems like a bit of an excursion, but our thinking on this idea is central to our holiness.

Every church establishes, intentionally or unintentionally, a meta-narrative about God and our interaction with him. This meta-narrative acts like a canvas on which the big, enduring truths about heaven, hell, sin, and salvation are painted. Let me explain. I spent my college years as part of a tightly knit InterVarsity Christian Fellowship campus group. Our crew attended a number of different churches in town on Sunday, one of which was a prominent Presbyterian congregation. My friends who went there loved it, and for good reason: the Bible was taught, God was worshiped, and people were excited about living for Jesus. It was a good church. That church's meta-narrative included, perhaps more prominently than any other subplot, the assurance that we humans are thoroughly, hopelessly, irretrievably sinful. The scriptural truth "For all have sinned and fall short of the glory of God" was trumpeted and drilled into the people, seemingly to underscore the glorious truth contained in the following verse: "And [all] are justified freely by his grace through the redemption that came by Christ Jesus."[1] The intense emphasis on grace produced an additional consequence, though: People felt less personal responsibility for their sin. *Aw, well, everybody does it, right? And like the preacher always says, I'm just a worthless wretched sinner,* the reasoning might go. It seems the meta-narrative of that church had convinced my Presbyterian friends that we can no more stop sinning than we can stop being human.

Others from our group went to a young, nondenominational charismatic church on the other side of town. They, too, loved their church, and with good reason: They were growing in passion for Jesus, praying hard, and motivating others to reach our campus with the gospel. The primary meta-narrative of that church, it seemed, was that as Christ's followers, we are overcomers—"a chosen people, a royal priesthood, a holy nation"[2]—and we have power over sin and the schemes of darkness because of Jesus. Like their Presbyterian friends, they rejoiced over the fact that "God made him who had no sin to be sin for us," but they held a stronger view of the corresponding promise "that in him we might become the righteousness of God."[3] My charismatic friends seemed decidedly more convinced that there was hope to stop sinning.

I pondered this question about sinning for several months before I came across a passage of Scripture that shed some light on the subject. The apostle John began his first letter to the fledgling Christian church with an eyewitness account of the Messiah. These verses intrigue me because they reflect the essence of Jesus's life and ministry as distilled by the man who was his closest friend. Imagine the wide-eyed wonder of the readers who had heard and believed and experienced profound transformation in their own lives but had never seen Jesus. John opened his account with these words:

> That which was from the beginning, which we have heard, which we have seen with our eyes, which we have looked at and our hands have touched—this we proclaim concerning the Word of life.

He continued on for the next four verses to build up the drama, and finally, he stated, "This is the message we have heard from him and declare to you: God is light; in him there is no darkness at all."[4]

I can just picture the befuddlement of these first-century believers: *God is light? That's the big revelation? That's the grand synopsis? You spent three years living and working with the man who's changed the hearts, stimulated the minds, freed the spirits, and captivated the imaginations of more people than anyone else in human history, and that's your prevailing impression?*

What seems too simple is actually the profoundest truth of our Savior, Immanuel, God-with-us. After three years' intimate contact with the author of the faith, John had figured out that Jesus and the Father are one. It was John's account that emphasized most heavily the reality that "anyone who has seen me has seen the Father."[5] And from Jesus's life and message, John concluded that God is holy, set apart, completely other. What he was trying to communicate about Jesus was mutual exclusivity: The nature of Jesus is such that he fundamentally cannot coexist with evil thoughts, desires, or tendencies. Jesus and sin are mutually exclusive. John was saying, in effect, "Young believers, the thing that was most astounding about being with Jesus—more than his humility or love or even his miracles—is that he did not sin!"

It's tempting to think, *Yeah, sure, but that was Jesus.* It's true, and with that we have to recognize that a crucial element of Jesus's ministry was to set an example for us. He defeated the devil in the wilderness not by summoning legions of warring angels but by quoting scripture he had memorized. He drove out demons not by baring his own holy arm but "by the finger of God,"[6] just as his disciples did. And he taught us to follow his lead. In his exhortation to a better righteousness in the Sermon on the Mount, Jesus made his expectation plain: "Be perfect…as your heavenly Father is perfect."[7]

In the text we started with, John acknowledged the reality of sin in believers' lives: "If we claim we have not sinned, we make him out to be a liar and his word has no place in our lives."[8] But he made it clear that sin is not normal for the Christian life, adding in the very next verse, "I write this to you so that you will not sin."[9] John affirmed Jesus's intention—"He appeared so that he might take away our sins"—and his legacy—"No one who lives in him keeps on sinning. No one who continues to sin has either seen him or known him."[10] If we have any hope of living into our calling, we have to understand that just as Jesus and sin cannot coexist, so it must increasingly be for his followers over the course of life.

Have Nothing to Do with Evil

I love the Psalms because they give insight into David's heart. It's interesting to read his poetry as you study this remarkable man because it affords a sort of between-the-lines commentary on his life. Nowhere is this phenomenon more vivid than in Psalm 101. Somewhere in the process of living into his calling as king, David realized that to succeed as king, he must wrestle with sin. Perhaps this happened when he was struggling with jealousy when his brothers were off fighting the Philistines and he was at home with the sheep. Or maybe it was after the episode with Bathsheba. Or it could have been after he had come all too close to wiping out Nabal and his household and bringing blood on his own head.

Whenever this happened, David evidently came to a place of clear decision as to who he was going to be, and he made a series of stunningly resolute vows. He resolved in his candid writing to be upright in his marriage and family (which suggests that he was writing in the wake of his adulterous affair with Bathsheba) and determined to "walk in my house with blameless heart." He pledged personal purity, vowing to "set before my eyes no vile thing." Not willing to stop halfway, David denounced even the savor of sin—"The deeds of faithless men I hate; they will not cling to me"—and rejected the company of those who would lead him that direction: "Men of perverse heart shall be far from me." Finally, in verse 4, he made a dramatic summary resolution: "I will have nothing to do with evil."[11]

David concluded this psalm with a charge to start holiness now. What he was saying, in effect, is "I will never again wait until I'm in the heat of the moment to decide. If I am trying to win the battle against sin while in the throes of temptation, I've already lost. If I get up to the brink and I haven't made a decision about my course, I've already decided."

David knew that God's plan for him included more—more opportunity, more responsibility, more blessing. He believed God's promises to him and anchored his hope firmly in that belief. He also knew, it seems, that walking deeper into his calling required stronger character, deeper conviction, more integrity, and greater purity. Implicit in David's decision to have nothing to do with evil was his awareness, his certainty, even, that advancement in his calling promised further—and likely more intense—temptation to sin. He knew the foolishness of assuming that he'd fight the escalated sin battle once he got there. One of our pastoral staff at New Life has a delightful ability to supply a catchy, corny aphorism to every situation. Here he might quip, "New levels, new devils!"

David highlighted the immeasurable value of those seasons of pretemptation lucidity—those windows of clarity—that we all have. To start living into our calling now, nothing is more foundational than capitalizing on these calms before life's inevitable storms of temptation. How I wish my boyhood pastor had thought about this.

Preemptive Holiness

If we are to adopt David's thinking and have nothing to do with evil, we need to make a holistic shift in our strategy. We've been waging war against sin from a passive, defensive posture, and we're losing. Day after day Christian brothers tell me how hard they're trying to resist the temptation to look at porn on the Internet and how miserably they're failing. Too many of us are getting slaughtered by the Enemy, falling and falling and falling into sin and effectively taking ourselves out of any real candidacy for advancement in the purposes of God. We're wasting the drive and talent God has entrusted to us by engaging in fruitless skirmishes, and we're losing too much ground. As if we're expecting an opponent who fights fair, we're waiting until the Enemy attacks and then trying to ward him off. But over and over again, he comes plowing through our front door with a backpack full of bombs.

David had a different idea of holiness. In much the same way that the administration of George W. Bush established a first-strike policy as America's defense platform in the war on terror, David suggested a personal doctrine of *preemptive holiness.*

Let me explain. It will take a while, but it will be worth it.

During the Cold War, the United States assumed a defensive military posture. The reasons for this are many, but here are perhaps the top three:

1. Our adversary was presumed to be rational. That is to say, it was considered safe to assume that the Soviet Union, though diametrically opposed to us ideologically, would operate in what it conceived to be the best interest of its people. It was further held to be true that the Soviets generally would not seek or advocate indiscriminate harm to people. They did have an agenda; they deeply believed in their socioeconomic ideas and wanted to foist them on other nations, no question about it. They wanted to redefine civilization, it is true, but they did not aspire to end it.

2. Mutual assured destruction. The blessing and curse of the Cold War was that the nuclear capabilities of the United States and the Soviet Union were public knowledge. The vast arsenal of munitions that each side possessed provided a weird global stability because everyone knew the grim reality of just how high the flames would rise once the first spark flew. If a first strike were launched, both sides knew that the only possible final state would be global thermonuclear holocaust. The high-stakes nature of the consequences of offensive action made a defensive posture the natural choice for rational states.

3. The battle was about ideas. No one during the Cold War really wanted to annihilate anyone else. What we really wanted to stamp out was each other's ideas. The standoff between the United States and the Soviet Union amounted to a tense, escalated conflict between radically different visions of civilization. The Soviet Union subscribed to Marx's concept of wealth distribution by a central power, while the United States and our Western allies adhered to Adam Smith's model of wealth creation in the free market. The Soviets believed that the state knows what is best for people, and the Americans believed that individuals are best suited to determine their own destiny. They believed that the role of government is to control; Americans believed it is to serve. The ideas were where the fault line lay. Nobody's primary objective was death or destruction, and so the conflict was naturally predisposed to a default posture of defense.

The archenemy to America and freedom-loving people around the world in the twenty-first century is quite different. Terrorists are anything but rational. Our enemies kill our noncombatants and their own—and they'll even kill themselves—and they seem to think nothing of it. No balance of power exists to provide stability. Terrorists know that we know that they know that we are stronger, so there is nothing to stay their hand. The fact that power is so asymmetric in this conflict emboldens our enemies, making them seemingly all too willing to go down in a blaze of glory. What is most subtle and dangerous about this conflict is that it is not an ideological one. It's masked in ideology, which makes it all the more insidious, but the terrorists' aim is not to convert us; it's to *kill* us.

For all these reasons, a defensive posture doesn't work as well against terrorists as it did against the Soviets. Thankfully, the Bush administration realized this and adopted the policy of preemption. We take the fight to them now. Our leaders decided that we prefer ferreting them out of rat holes in Fallujah over guessing which 7-Eleven in Toledo, Ohio, they might walk into with a bomb strapped around their waist. During the Cold War, we would watch and wait for the enemy's incursion into an area like Korea or Vietnam or Cuba and then match their actions with measured responses. Now we go out looking for terrorists and defeat them before they can ever attack.

Now for the part where you stop asking, "What in the world?" and all this ties together and starts making sense.

Why We're Losing

Our war with the enemy of our souls goes the same way. Too many of us have mischaracterized our adversary. We're trying to wage twentieth-century-style warfare in the twenty-first century. We're opposing Osama bin Laden the same way we opposed the Soviet Union during the Cold War, and it's not working. Look at it this way: Our enemy is no more rational than the terrorists who fly themselves into our buildings. In fact, he is far less so. Not only is he willing to inflict collateral damage, but he's hoping to. You can bet he will catch in the cross fire as many women, children, churches, hospitals, and Red Cross facilities as he can. He thrives on the thought of taking you down, shaming your mother, bankrupting your father, and disillusioning your friends in the process. Just like the terrorists, our enemy knows there is no balance of power. He knows all too well that God is more powerful. He was there at the Resurrection. He's not interested in détente, because he has nothing to conserve, no equal footing to lose, and so he goes all-out. And like the terrorists, his purpose is not ideology but destruction. He's not satisfied to persuade you; he wants to consume you.

We have adopted a theology—by default, really—that tells us to resist temptation and flee from the Enemy. We take a passive defensive posture against the devil, knowing and talking with our accountability groups about the ways he might attack us but waiting until he strikes to engage him. We live along like this, and one day, inevitably—*smack!*—he jumps out of the bushes like Mel Gibson and his band of guerrilla patriots against the militarily superior but unsuspecting British regiment, and he goes to school on our booty. We have the tools to win, but we choose not to use them. Instead, we like to walk around in dangerous territory until we get pounced on, and then we feebly try to fight back once we do. This is a foolish way to fight our enemy, and sadly, the results are that too many of God's people get derailed from their callings or wrecked altogether.

The Line

When I worked with high schoolers, the question kids asked me most often was, "Where's the line?" You know, *the line.* How far can I go and still be okay with God? Can I kiss her on the mouth? If I can kiss her on the mouth, can I French-kiss her? If I can French-kiss her, can I snuggle on the couch with her? If I can snuggle on the couch with her, can I touch her outside her clothes? Can I touch her stomach under her shirt? Can I touch her breasts? Can I take her clothes off as long as we don't have sex? How far can I go?

They all wanted me to tell them the same thing: how close they could get to the red-hot burner of sin without scorching their fingers. They all knew since Sunday school that they were to avoid the wicked deeds of darkness, and they genuinely wanted to serve God. They thought that if someone would just tell them where the line was, they could stay safely on this side of it and be okay. So they would find someone or some book that would say the line is *here,* and then they would live right up to the line. Many would conclude that the line is French kissing, and they would maraud their date's tonsils until the poor girl was forced to defend her lips. Others would determine the line to be snuggling. The trouble is that they could invariably be found, before too long, entwined in a kind of "snuggling" that more resembled Hulk Hogan's legendary Wrestlemania III defeat of Andre the Giant than anything remotely romantic.

That's always the problem with living close to the line: You always want to go further. We've learned to stand on the edge and peek over, and we like what we've seen. Over time we end up in the awkward and unsustainable position of living with our bodies on this side of the line—no *touching* her breast, no *ordering* a drink, no *telling* coarse jokes, whatever—but our minds squarely on the other side. When we live close to the line and look over the edge, the impulse that drew our bodies to the line always drags our minds across it. I never met a young man who lived close to the line and didn't struggle with thoughts of crossing it.

Too many of us live our lives this way. We look for someone who will tell us where the line is, and we'll get as close to that line as we possibly can and settle down and live there. I see it over and over again. We seek out an exact placement of the line in the name of a holiness that bears no resemblance at all to God's design. Supposing our responsibility to be to resist temptation, we position ourselves squarely in the Enemy's kill zone, sit up nice and tall for him to train his sights on us, and live out our lives there. We might as well affix a huge red bull's-eye to our backsides. He lets us camp out there for a while, get comfortable, convince ourselves that we are ably resisting his nefarious designs, and then lower our guard a little. Then he hits us. Like the ragtag and unorthodox colonial militia against the vastly superior British regiment, he swoops in and overpowers us because we are close in and we don't have time to get our muskets loaded and get in position. We let our underpowered adversary defeat us again and again with his archaic spears and hatchets while our bullets and gunpowder sit idly by. We lose by stupidly walking into his ambush, nullifying our military advantage, and delivering ourselves to him on a silver platter. Our resistance proves futile against the sudden, barbaric, and overwhelming onslaught of his temptation, and we fall headlong right over the line.

Once we've tried and failed to resist temptation because we've faced off against the Enemy on his home turf and in his preferred style of combat, what have we left to do but run away bleating? We fail and we fall and then, of course, we flee. And this completes the cycle: Overpowered and embarrassed, we run away from the Enemy we're supposed to be putting to flight and instead go whimpering back to our accountability groups where we confess yet again how we messed up. If the devil can't have our souls, his next preference is to leave us weak and powerless and consumed with our own inability not to blow it. What a shame that over and over throughout our lives, we encounter the enemy of our souls, that ancient foe whose intent and tactics have been made plain to us, whose inferiority we have time and again confidently pronounced, of whose ultimate resounding and final defeat we definitively know…and we run away with our tails between our legs! This is a travesty!

If we are going to live into the calling of God on our lives, we must figure out how to get out of this perpetual cycle of impotence. So why do so many of us keep failing? Why do we lose battles again and again to an enemy armed with hatchets when we have guns and explosives at our disposal? This is the question David figured out, and the answer is preemptive holiness.

What Are We Resisting and What Are We Fleeing?

We lose our battles because we have believed a fundamentally wrong idea. So many of us have cultivated a personal theology of resisting temptation and fleeing the Enemy when this is not at all what God intends. God's idea is for us to *flee temptation and resist the Enemy.* Let me explain.

Of course we all have to deal with temptation; there is no way out of that. But look at what the Bible says about it. In his comments about the Corinthian believers' temptation to return to their former sexual perversions, the apostle Paul instructed the church, "*Flee* from sexual immorality."[12] And later, concerning the tempting trend of making idols, he added,

> So, if you think you are standing firm, be careful that you don't fall! No temptation has seized you except what is common to man. And God is faithful; he will not let you be tempted beyond what you can bear. But when you are tempted, he will also provide a way out so that you can stand up under it. Therefore, my dear friends, *flee* from idolatry.[13]

To his pupil Timothy concerning the allure of riches, the apostle commented,

> People who want to get rich fall into temptation and a trap and into many foolish and harmful desires that plunge men into ruin and destruction. For the love of money is a root of all kinds of evil. Some people, eager for money, have wandered from the faith and pierced themselves with many griefs. But you, man of God, *flee* from all this.[14]

And, again, later in his letter, Paul encouraged his protégé in the face of the temptations especially familiar to young men: "*Flee* the evil desires of youth."[15]

Flee, flee, flee. Over and over again, the Scriptures instruct us in no uncertain terms that we ought not to be trying to figure out how close we can get to the line; we ought to be turning tail and running the other direction from it! We are foolish to think that it is honorable to live at the devil's doorstep and fight against yielding to his dastardly wiles. There is no honor there! Choosing to live on the line and constantly struggling to resist temptation wastes your life. You spin your wheels fast and loud, but you never make any forward progress because you can't get any traction. Too many of us have been living this one-step-forward, one-step-back life for too long. We need to change our thinking.

When his disciples asked him how they ought to pray, Jesus himself underscored this crucial idea. After instructing them to ask for forgiveness for their sins, he continued, "And lead us not into temptation."[16] Notice that Jesus specifically did not tell them to ask the Father, "Help us resist temptation" or "Aid us in the fight against temptation" or "Defeat temptation for us." He told them instead to ask to be led around it. In effect, this was his message: *Ask God to show you where the line is, and then go the other way. Petition him for the bypass route so you never have to encounter the fault line between right and wrong and use your frail human will to resist the temptation that being near that line produces in people. Flee temptation.*

Again to his disciples, this time in the Garden of Gethsemane on the eve of his execution, Jesus said, "Watch and pray so that you will not fall into temptation. The spirit is willing, but the body is weak."[17] Do you see it? Jesus was telling them to look out for where temptation may lie and to go the other way. Why? Because even though your spirit would like to resist temptation and choose godliness, your flesh is weak. Choosing to face temptation is not the wisest path because you are too susceptible to giving in to it.

This idea resonates throughout the Bible. Many of us have come to think that we're doing the right thing when we're trying to resist sinful acts, but the Bible counsels us not to resist them but to "have nothing to do with the fruitless deeds of darkness."[18] We think we are on the right track when we are trying not to give in to evil, but the Bible instructs us not just to avoid participating in it but to hate evil.[19] As we saw before, David made that critical determination in Psalm 101: "I will have nothing to do with evil."

So why do so many of us choose to have a little something to do with evil without actually doing the evil? Simple: because we still like it. We give up the *act* of sinning because there's motivation to. The Bible makes clear that "neither the sexually immoral nor idolaters nor adulterers nor male prostitutes nor homosexual offenders nor thieves nor the greedy nor drunkards nor slanderers nor swindlers will inherit the kingdom of God."[20] And let's be honest. Now that we've come to believe in eternal punishment, we all want to go to heaven. We have sufficient motivation not to continue engaging bodily in sin the way we used to. Ah, but how sweet it is. What a fortunate refuge for our sin-starved flesh to be able to continue *thinking* about it! Hey, check this out: I can be saved from punishment by not actually doing the stuff, but I can live right on the edge of the stuff and still see it and smell it and almost taste it. People live on the line because they still like the sin.

In ninth-grade English, my class had to read Homer's *Odyssey.* (I say "had to" because in my fifteen-year-old mind, reading a 650-page poem fell on the list of things I least wanted to do in life, somewhere just below spending the afternoon with my mother in Hobby Lobby or watching *The Sound of Music* with my family for the ninth Christmas in a row. Now, though, *The Sound of Music* is great fun in my home because it's Mauri's favorite movie in all the world, and so I can really get her lathered up when I say, "I can't believe he doesn't end up choosing the baroness—she's not ornery like Maria, she's far hotter, and she doesn't do silly, free-spirited things like cutting up Captain von Trapp's curtains.") Anyway, we read the *Odyssey*, and in spite of myself, I ended up liking it. The part of Odysseus's adventure I remember most vividly is his encounter with the Sirens. As ships passed their island, these creatures would sing their haunting and enchanting songs. Many vessels were lost and many crewmen died because the Sirens' song was so alluring and so powerful.

Odysseus, being more cunning than the captains who had passed the Sirens before him, learned of the creatures' sinister scheme and determined not to let his men fall under their spell. Still, Odysseus was so intrigued by the legend of the Sirens' song that he ordered his men to tie him to the mast as they approached the island. Every member of his crew was to stuff his ears with beeswax, and Odysseus alone was to hear the Sirens' song. He made his men swear an oath that no matter how he pleaded, ranted, or insisted, they would not under any circumstances untie him from the mast. And so it happened. Bound tightly to the ship, Odysseus heard the Sirens, and indeed he did plead, rant, and order his men to untie him. That's just the way we are with sin. We know to avoid engaging in it, but too many of us want to experience it just a little, to be near it and take in the aroma and be tickled by its hypnotic allure, hoping vainly that we're going to stay fastened to the frail mast of our own resolve.

The Two Losses

There is a subtle but vitally important distinction between resisting the deeds of darkness and having nothing to do with them, between not sinning and hating the idea of sin. In both cases, our bodies are not engaging in the sin. The difference lies in what our minds are doing. The apostle Paul gave an insightful statement about his own faith journey in his letter to the Philippians:

> I consider everything a loss compared to the surpassing greatness of knowing Christ Jesus my Lord, for whose sake I have lost all things. I consider them rubbish, that I may gain Christ.[21]

Notice that Paul testified to losing two things: the physical, bodily loss of earthly pleasures and the emotional loss of enjoying thinking about them. He not only "lost all things," but he "consider[ed] them rubbish" after making the decision not to participate in them bodily. We may suffer the first loss, but too many of us stop short of the second one. The result is that we suffer the loss, as it were, of sinful pleasures, but we continue allowing ourselves to think they're nice rather than thinking they're rubbish. We give up sinful living outwardly, but inside we still cherish it. That's what draws us to the line. We assume a look-but-don't-touch attitude, and we find ourselves attracted to the very worldliness we are supposed to have nothing to do with. We savor the idea of the evil we should hate, and we put ourselves in temptation's line of fire.

You can see these two losses throughout David's life. Not only had he concluded that he wouldn't engage in sin—"I will walk in my house with blameless heart"—but he wouldn't even *set before his eyes* anything vile. Not only would he not join in with people who were sinning—"The deeds of faithless men I hate"—but he determined that perverse men *"shall be far from me."* And as I pointed out before, not only did he choose to avoid participating in sinful activities, but he resolutely vowed to "have nothing to do with evil."[22] David decided as a young man to suffer the loss of sinful living, for sure, but he also chose to give up the idea of sin's attractiveness. He endured both losses, and that's what it takes to flee temptation.

Chapter 11

Living at the Devil's Doorstep (and Running Away Like a Squealing Schoolgirl)

Look...everyone in this room knows what people are saying about our chances. I know it. You know it. But I also know there is a way to stay with this team. You don't defend them—you *attack* them. You take their game and you shove it right back in their face. The team that is finally willing to do this is the team that has a chance to put them down.

—COACH HERB BROOKS to the 1980 U.S. Olympic hockey team prior to the semifinal game against the Soviet Union, from the movie *Miracle*

If we play our game and not theirs, we'll win.

—every professional athlete ever interviewed before a big game

Okay, so we've established that many try to resist temptation when God's idea is for us to flee. The other half of this idea is that, as a result of our living near sin and trying to resist it, we end up fleeing from the Enemy when we're supposed to be resisting him.

I remember as a boy going outside on summer evenings after dinner and meeting up with the other kids in the neighborhood to play "ghost in the graveyard." The premise was that one kid would be the ghost and would go hide somewhere, and everyone else had to look for him. When they found him, he would chase after them, and they would try to run away. It became a game of tag, with the ghost being "it" and the searchers trying to reach the safety of the base before getting tagged. (It's kind of absurd if you think about it. What is the motivation to go looking for the ghost? You might as well just hang around the base, since you're just going to run away frantically as soon as you see him anyway.)

Silly as it sounds, this is the way many of us approach the enemy of our souls. Liking the idea of sin causes us to creep around, half looking for the one we know is out to destroy us. The same senseless appeal that made us kids want to find the very one we did not want to find motivates us to get as close to the line as we can, and then, ultimately, inevitably—*Boo!*—out he jumps from inside the bushes or behind the fence, and we squeal like schoolchildren and run away. We try to resist when we're supposed to flee, and we end up fleeing when we're supposed to resist.

Scripture is unmistakably clear as to our role vis-à-vis the Enemy. Over and over again it exhorts us to resist the devil and his army of darkness. That is not to say the devil is not formidable. Many godly people have come to rue the fact that they once underestimated his power. No, he is not impotent. Jesus taught his followers that the Enemy "comes only to steal and kill and destroy."[1] Concerning the devil and his nefarious designs, the apostle Peter wrote, "Be self-controlled and alert. Your enemy the devil prowls around like a roaring lion looking for someone to devour." But wait—the instruction doesn't end there! Jesus's friend continued on to say, "*Resist him,* standing firm in the faith."[2] Not only does the Bible make no mention of our backing down from our adversary, but it instructs us to stand up and fight. And not only does it say nothing about our running away, but it teaches that when we do our job—"Resist the devil"—the opposite will happen: "*He* will flee from *you.*"[3]

This is a huge idea and a fundamental paradigm shift for many American Christians. We presuppose that, at the end of the day, Satan is stronger than we are, and so we live our ghost-in-the-graveyard Christianity and give the devil power and authority that are not his. Didn't you know that "you…are from God and have overcome [Satan and his demons]?" You are not in the process of overcoming the devil. You are not destined to overcome him someday. You don't have to hope or wish or live in anticipation of overcoming him. You have overcome him already, "because the one who is in you is greater than the one who is in the world."[4]

Greater means "larger in size; larger in quantity or number; more remarkable or outstanding in magnitude, degree, or extent; of more outstanding significance or importance; superior in quality or character; more powerful; more influential; more imminent; more distinguished." Greater. So here's the point: Left to our own devices, the devil wins; relying on Christ in us, though, we dominate.

Too many of us have it flat-out backward. We are trying to fight what we should be running from and trying to run from what we should be fighting. Why is this happening? Why are we living on the line and putting ourselves in the position of having to play the Enemy's game when we know we will win playing ours?

Getting Off Our Game

In 1985 the Boston Celtics were the best team in basketball. Larry Bird was in his prime (he won one of his six Most Valuable Player awards that season), the offense was a well-oiled machine, and the bench was strong. (Actually, the bench wasn't that strong, but the offense was a well-oiled machine.) The New England area suffered a collective heartbreak that year when the Celtics lost to the dreaded Los Angeles Lakers in the NBA Championship—a wound, like Frodo's piercing at the hands of the Nazgûl, that I will carry with me forever. Losing itself was painful; it was all the worse because the Celtics were, by every estimation, the superior team that year. When they played their game—slow the ball, use the clock, run the half-court offense, and shoot the lights out—no team could stop them. They lost the championship because the Lakers flustered them, got them off their game, and took control. The Celts didn't set the tempo; the Lakers did. The Celts didn't choose the style of play; the Lakers did. In the whirlwind of fast breaks, fast ball movement, and fast scoring, the Celtics broke down and came unglued. More frustrating from the fans' perspective than the loss itself was that, at any moment, at whatever juncture they chose, Boston could have taken control. Our heroes in green could have stopped playing their opponent's game and started playing their own. They could have won if they had played to their strengths, but instead they resigned themselves to playing the Lakers's brand of ball, and they got stomped.

This is exactly what happens to us in our fight with the devil, and it costs far too many people their callings. When we choose to live close to the line, we put ourselves at such a disadvantage that we have no hope of winning. And it's such a shame because we are the better team by far! We have all the tools we need to win, you see, but only if we play our game rather than getting sucked into our adversary's.

Why Can't We Learn from Vietnam?

When I was a tank platoon leader, I learned the value of exploiting your superiority. The United States Army is equipped with the M1A2 Abrams Main Battle Tank, the finest heavy weaponry in all of mechanized warfare. Our guns can shoot farther, penetrate deeper, and kill more than anything else on the battlefield. Our night-vision capability enables American soldiers to detect enemy combatants in the dark sooner than any of our adversaries can. What's more, our indirect fire, close air support, and satellite intelligence enable our troops to engage the enemy miles before he can even detect us. Rest assured, we are superior on the battlefield.

During my first rotation through the National Training Center (this is the official-sounding name for the aforementioned desolate, depressing, and unimaginably hot piece of desert somewhere between Los Angeles and Las Vegas where we go to have fake tank battles and to overcome the innate, subconscious fear of scorpions and other scary desert-dwelling reptiles and arachnids—a fear that lurks in all of us), I made the classic rookie mistake. Zealous to engage the enemy, I took my platoon of four tanks out of our assigned support position overlooking the engagement area and charged into the enemy's kill zone. This was stupid because (1) it left our sister platoon without a base of supporting fire for its assault on the enemy position, and (2) my frenetic battle charge took away our military superiority. The point of positioning ourselves two kilometers away was to exploit the superior range of our guns and night-vision devices and to give us time to react to the enemy's maneuvering. Instead, I turned our advantages into disadvantages: The slow-moving gun turret and limited view of a tank at close range could not track the enemy's highly mobile ground forces, the close range took away any reaction time to enemy fire, and our lumbering, sixty-three-ton silhouettes were easy prey for a shoulder-fired antitank rocket. Not only was it disappointing that our whole platoon was wiped out, but it was wiped out by only two foot soldiers with a weapon whose range couldn't even reach our original position. We forfeited our superiority and made ourselves susceptible to the enemy's surprise attack. We got sucked into playing his game.

This was the problem in the Vietnam War. No, the problem with the Vietnam War was that we elected Lyndon Johnson instead of Barry Goldwater in 1964. But what I'm talking about here is the problem with our *strategy* for conducting the war: We forfeited our vastly superior military capability and got sucked instead into close-range ground combat in terrain that was foreign to us and familiar to the Vietcong. We conceded to playing their game rather than our own, and the results were thousands of lives needlessly lost and a permanent stain on the record of the mighty American military.

The problem with living close to sin and looking over the edge is that it invariably puts us in a position of having to resist temptation, and it inhibits our capacity to resist the Enemy. It's a double whammy, as it requires us to do what we're *not* made to do and limits our ability to do what we *are* made to do. When we plant ourselves right next to sin, we take away our time to react to the enemy. We forfeit the capability of scanning the horizon, seeking out the enemy, and systematically, matter-of-factly annihilating him. Instead, we relegate ourselves to close-range fighting. Where we should be finding and destroying the enemy, we instead subject ourselves to his ambush. It's only a matter of time before temptation jumps out of the bushes, pounces on us, and plunders us. Our superior weaponry is useless at such close range, and we have no choice but to run away.

If It's So Counterproductive, Why Do We Do It?

Why do so many of us get inverted like this? Over the years of sitting and listening to people's perpetual struggles with sin, watching them lick their wounds after getting trampled by the Enemy, and talking through these ideas with them, I've distilled several common reasons people live so close to the line. Here are four:

1. Cheap grace. Many of us have bought into a lie somewhere along the path of our Christian journey. We've allowed ourselves to become convinced that grace is a sort of spiritual get-out-of-jail-free card. In *The Cost of Discipleship,* Dietrich Bonhoeffer wrote:

> Cheap grace is the deadly enemy of our Church. We are fighting to-day for costly grace.
>
> Cheap grace means grace sold on the market like cheapjacks' wares. The sacraments, the forgiveness of sin, and the consolations of religion are thrown away at cut prices. Grace is represented as the Church's inexhaustible treasury, from which she showers blessings with generous hands, without asking questions or fixing limits. Grace without price; grace without cost! The essence of grace, we suppose, is that the account has been paid in advance; and, because it has been paid, everything can be had for nothing.[5]

Too many of us have let ourselves believe in grace as the big cover-up. Cheap grace allows for—even endorses—living close to the line because its primary purpose is to get us out of the jam we put ourselves in every time we fall into sin. Cheap grace exists so we can sin and sin and then be sorry and make it all okay. It requires no inner transformation, just acknowledgment that God loves us, wretches though we are, and has provided perma-forgiveness through the blood of Jesus. There is no repentance, no turning the other way—just sinning and apologizing.

Where did we get this idea? Perhaps we were taught it in some church somewhere or we've watched it lived out in front of us—or maybe we just created a personal theology to accommodate our sin preferences. However we learned it, we believe it because we want to believe it. We like having a license to be weak, to stumble, to fall, and to fail. We like cheap grace because it requires little of us beyond some semblance of sincerity. We can have our cake and eat it too—and do it all in the name of a mighty, loving God who is strong when we are weak.

When I was in college, some of my friends joined a church in town that was very doctrinally correct. After a semester of attending those services, students could recite and argue reformed theology, enumerate Calvin's countertheses to the remonstrants, and summarize the conclusions of the Council of Dort. The trouble was that many who were so assured of their own election and others' reprobation, so convinced of their own and everyone else's inability to do anything good, and so persuaded of God's endless flow of weakness-pardoning grace were also sadly lacking in much of the fruit of repentance. To this crowd, teaching on holiness was legalism. Seeking victory over sin was pride. Living close to the line became a self-fulfilling prophecy of repeatedly battling and losing to the inevitable temptation that comes from living there and then pointing to the struggle as evidence of their interminable weakness and desperate need of grace. This crowd preferred the cycle of falling headlong into sin, crying noisily about their weakness, and receiving cheap grace over having to do anything about it.

2. Phony relevance. It has become popular for church people to talk about relevance. Postmoderns, they say, are looking for authenticity above all else, and consequently many churches are running to the dime store and buying anything relevant. Pastors across America are growing goatees, wearing jeans and Doc Martens, preaching sermon series like "Authentic Faith," and talking about their weaknesses from the pulpit—all in the name of relevance.

An interesting side effect has resulted from so many sensible churches' journey to relevance—it would be comical if its consequences weren't so dire. Relevant church is shaping its congregants' values. Just the way McDonald's can spend billions of dollars every year convincing America that an amalgam of mysterious products loosely identifiable as meat and molded into a patty resembling a small rack of ribs is appetizing, cool church is shaping its consumers' appetite. Cool church gathers Gen Xers and others who identify with postmodern culture and drills into them that their highest values are authenticity and relevance, giving birth to a group mentality in which being real trumps all. We're creating another self-fulfilling prophecy, and the unintended consequence is hordes of Christian twentysomethings who live on the line and use "cultural relevance" as their justification.

Several years ago, before I was pastoring at New Life Church, some friends of mine chose a different path than I did. They started attending a church where the pastor was real (he talked a lot about his struggles) and the people were authentic (they didn't judge you for playing with sin). I didn't hear much from them until a few years later when I started receiving prayer requests (that's the way to gossip when you're a Christian) from deeply concerned intercessors for my relevant friends and their drinking habit. Going to bars and doing shots, having beer at their Bible studies, getting drunk on New Year's Eve—the reports kept pouring in. What had gotten into my friends? They were convinced they had become relevant. Being cool and in touch with culture made living close to the line seem okay to them.

Cool church is hurting the cause of Christ. Of course, there is nothing wrong with doing church and trying to make it cool. The problem arises—and it inevitably does arise—when our priorities fall out in this order: (1) cool; (2) church. Ultimately, the two ideals collide. We're going to be faced with the conundrum of something that is innately *church* being profoundly uncool and something else that is supremely *cool* being foundationally unchurch. Cool church works when it's pillar candles, Starbucks coffee, and oriental rugs hanging from the wall. It gets sketchier when it's worship by walking through a labyrinth or a wind tunnel, and it falls apart when it's Bibles and Beer. Insofar as cool church takes the core ideas of obedience to Scripture, corporate worship, and fellowship with believers and packages them in a way that is palatable to non-insiders, it has great value. But too often, cool church becomes more about *cool* than *church,* and the upshot is compromising that which should be resolute. Cool church done badly lifts the skirts of God's people in front of a world waiting to denigrate us at any opportunity.

Ted Haggard, my pastor, mentor, and friend, once said something that has stuck with me through my years of pastoring. In explaining to me the importance of working with the secular media to portray New Life and the American church in the most positive light, Pastor Ted told me, "I'm jealous for the reputation of the bride of Christ." Well, years have passed, and I find myself jealous for the reputation of the church in my generation. Christ intended for his body to portray him—the one in whom the fullness of the Godhead was pleased to dwell bodily—to a lost and dying world. Sure, let's lose some of the exclusive, arcane, churchy packaging that has been so off-putting to the secular public. Absolutely, let's present Christ in cultural context and break down traditional barriers that have kept people from approaching our great source of hope. Redress God's favorite institution, but do it with kid gloves. It's not the many and varied attempts to make the church cool that are troubling to me; it's the flippant dismissal in the process of any of that ancient fear of the Lord that laid out Moses, put woe into Isaiah, caused Martin Luther to doubt his own salvation, sent William Carey to India, and drove my grandmother to her knees in prayer every day of her life. How lightly we let go of the love of purity! It's great to be relevant, but in our extreme makeover of the glorious gospel of our salvation, we must never forget that we are the light of the world, and where the light is, the darkness cannot remain.

3. Ad hoc holiness. One of the emblems of my childhood is Chuck E. Cheese. I remember my delight while navigating the maze of video games, Skee-Ball lanes, motorized life-size dancing rodents, and the try-to-grab-a-plush-toy-that-is-worth-less-than-the-quarter-you-paid-to-play mechanical arm machines. Chuck E. Cheese was enough to stimulate every nerve of any ten-year-old. I was particularly fond of the Whack a Mole game. Remember? There were six holes and a padded mallet with which, to my parents' dismay, I took considerably greater delight whacking my sister than the moles that popped up randomly and briefly in the holes. Of course, the more moles you whacked, the more tickets you earned toward the purchase of said cheap-o plush toys and other worthless junk. So the game went like this: You'd stand in front of the machine, watching for a mole to pop up, and then try to whack it when it did.

That's the way many of us approach the sin in our lives. Rather than identifying the Enemy's footholds and forcefully ripping them out, we sit back and wait for sinful tendencies to manifest themselves, and then we try to whack them back down. We allow ourselves to become content treating the symptoms of sin rather than going after the root cause. The problem with Whack-a-Mole holiness is that it's ad hoc—the sin nature is in control, and we simply respond to its whims and wiles. The result is that we never overcome. There is no victory. We stay chained to our sinful habits and desires, trying desperately and vainly to whack the sin back down after it comes to the surface and hurtling ever faster toward self-destruction.

If you think about it, this is the problem the free world is facing with terrorism. The way the American Civil Liberties Union would have us fight the war on terror, we would sit back and wait for the broiling underworld of fundamentalist hatred to project its will on innocent, defenseless free people—whenever, wherever, and however it chooses—and respond with public outrage afterward. Then we'd try to figure out who did it and who planned it and how they got the weapons and how they gained access to our country, embassy, building, airplane, or whatever. We'd arrest a few fringe participants because the triggermen are all dead and the masterminds are hiding in rugged, undetectable caves in central Asia (taking great care, naturally, not to infringe on the Miranda rights of these illegal-immigrant, noncitizen criminals); initiate some congressional inquiries; commission an independent investigating committee to write a bestseller; point out the flaws in the sitting president's administration; and wait for the next attack, as all the while the nation grows less secure and more paralyzed with fear. This approach sounds good to some because it protects people's rights. No one is subject to any imposition. But the problem is that everyone gets worse off.

I meet people every week who have unwittingly subscribed to Whack-a-Mole holiness. They have clearly identified the holes in their lives that sin will pop out of—pornography or anger or jealousy or whatever—and they have positioned themselves vigilantly over the holes to swipe at the sin once it rears its ugly head. They typically go to accountability groups and talk about how they sinned, repent of the sin at the altar with fanfare and wailing, and wallow in shame and regret over the sin until the sin and their reaction to it end up defining them. The trouble is, they never address the root cause. Whack-a-Mole Christians are chronically unwilling to look deep inside themselves, identify sin's secret source, invite the illumination of the Holy Spirit, and roll up their sleeves and go to work on it. Whack-a-Mole holiness is like trying to get the weeds out of your flower bed but not wanting to get your hands dirty—you end up waiting till the weeds sprout, grabbing them by the tops, and yanking out the blades. Everything looks better for a while, but the weeds just grow right back because you didn't dig in and pull up the roots.

Whack-a-Mole holiness invariably leads to living close to the line. People who follow Christ this way don't actively resist the Enemy, and so they passively aid him. Sin encroaches in our hearts like the tide coming in, each wave advancing farther up the beach, erasing previous watermarks and leaving once-dry land under water. Without active resistance, the devil keeps taking ground. We don't usually choose to march on up to the line and defiantly camp there; instead, we find that after each successive bout with sin, our inhibition has shrunk, our tolerance has grown, and our shoreline has eroded just a little bit. And one day we wake up to find that we've been living close to the line for some time. With a twinge of sadness, we resign ourselves to the reality that the line now defines us.

4. A well-managed portfolio. This reason why people live close to the line and play into the Enemy's hand is similar to the previous one, but with one important distinction. Whereas Whack-a-Molers, by default, treat the symptoms of sin without addressing the cause, sin portfolio managers live this way as a calculated choice. They are smart, and they've figured out the game. They think they can beat the house, but they're wrong.

I've met a number of people over the past few years who are interested in heaven, blessing, and relationships with God's people—on their terms. Like the Whack-a-Molers, these sin mitigators are earnest in identifying the areas of weakness in their lives, vigilant in learning the pathway that temptation uses to get to them, and deft at planning sin-management strategies. They create a sort of sin portfolio, watching for dips and spikes and keeping everything under control—or so the devil allows them to believe. One sin asset dips into the trouble zone, and they give attention to it, supposing they can level it out. The other areas, they presume, are okay as long as they're not flaring up. Sin-portfolio managers approach godliness with the brazen misunderstanding that they, on their own, are more powerful than the enemy of their souls.

The classic example of sin management is young men who masturbate. Having spent hundreds of hours talking with young masturbators over the years, I've become something of a de facto field expert on the subject. My contention is that masturbation is one manifestation of what the Bible calls sexual immorality: sexual activity outside of God's parameters. Scripture prohibits fornication, adultery, orgies, homosexual sex, and bestiality because they fall outside the confines of God's intent for sexuality. Masturbation is sin for the same reason; it's sex with oneself. God's idea of sexuality is one man and one woman in the confines of a marriage covenant: "For this reason a man will leave his father and mother and be united to his wife, and the two will become one flesh."[6]

Some respected theories out there argue that masturbation is fine so long as it is not accompanied by lustful thoughts. While this may be theoretically true, young men know that it's practically irrelevant; they know that divorcing the act from the thought is about as hopeful a solution as negotiating with a union. They know masturbation is sin. The challenge has never been to convince them that masturbation displeases God, but rather to change their thinking about how to confront this insidious issue. Young men always want to check in with others who share the struggle, to keep tabs, to report stats. They reason that if they are honest with people about the fact that they masturbate, they can keep it under control. It's sin management.

Now let me qualify my comments on masturbation. In all my years of ministering to young men, I have known two who have never masturbated, and I know one other person who has done it just once. That is three out of hundreds. Does that make it okay? I mean, hey, everyone does it, right? No way. Despite what people tell you, no sin is justified simply because a lot of people are struggling with it. But at the same time, does the ubiquity of this issue mean that all those who struggle are doomed, that they have no hope for redemption? Certainly not! I know many, many men who have overcome the temptation to masturbate, and I know many more who are gaining mastery over it. There is hope, there is redemption, and—trust me, my friend—there is freedom. Stay the course, flee temptation, resist the Enemy, and follow Christ to victory.

Portfolio managers live close to the line because they like it there. Never fully submitting to Christ's lordship, they buy the devil's tawdry line that he is not really interested in possessing them; he just wants to make them a little bit bad. Wittingly or unwittingly, they strike a deal with the dark one and naively believe he is going to keep his end of the bargain.

Listen to me: The devil will not work with you to find the custom-tailored sin level of your preference. He has no interest in helping you maintain a "sin life" that's under control. He wants to destroy you to the utmost. He is crafty, though. He will allow you to believe you are successfully managing your sin life for a time, long enough to set the hook firmly, and then he will bring you down. The devil will never work with you; he will only work against you. If he seems to be accommodating your preferred degree of sinfulness and not asking anything more, it's because he wants to lull you into living on the line. He wants to set you up in the middle of his kill zone—slow, fat, and comfortable with a bull's-eye target hanging around your neck—and then, at some opportune time when you think you have everything under control, utterly decimate you.

The Enemy operates like a casino. The casino is happy for you to believe that you have a good chance of winning. They will even give you free drinks while you sit back down to play just one more round, but they are fully aware that the longer you stay, the worse off you get, because, in the long run, *the house always wins.* Well, be assured that when you play the devil's game, dabble with sin, and think you can keep yourself from getting sucked in, you are dead wrong. God didn't design you to have a sin life. When you live near the line and play around with sin and think you can keep it from getting out of hand, you're living in a fog. If you're living this way, you are walking down the devil's primrose path, and it won't be long before he finds the perfect moment to bring everything crashing down around you.

■ ■ ■

Okay, wow. That was heavy. I need to take a deep breath now because I'm fired up and the veins in my neck are bulging a bit. But before I end this chapter, I need to ask you a critical question. If you're convinced that it's futile to abandon your weapons and run into the Enemy's kill zone, if you believe that we lose before we start when we resist what we should be fleeing and flee what we should be resisting, the question is, *How, then, do we resist the devil?*

Now is the time to learn the answer to this question. Now, while we are living into our calling. Now, before the heat is on. Now is the time to start fighting. Now is the time to learn how to wield the inestimably great power entrusted to us, and now is the time to start making the Enemy miserable. So, how do we do it?

Chapter 12

What's in You Is What'll Come Out of You

My momma always said, "Life is like a box of chocolates. You never know what you're gonna get. . . ."

Momma always says there's an awful lot you could tell about a person by their shoes. . . .

Now, my momma always told me that miracles happen every day. Some people don't think so, but they do. . . .

Momma always said that God is mysterious. . . .

My momma always said you got to put the past behind you before you can move on.

—FORREST GUMP

As David stood across the field from the giant warrior, his life must have flashed before him. This was his moment, the culmination of his entire life so far. Both armies watched, incredulous, a thousand cynical quips at the ready. The king puffed himself and scoffed dismissively for the benefit of the aides around him, and secretly he stewed over who this boy was, what it would mean if he was cut to pieces, and what it would mean if he somehow prevailed. An enormous man who was highly trained in combat and weaponry stood on the battlefield mocking and deriding, fully expecting in a few moments' time to be towering over one more dead body. The moment was a lifetime of tension:

> The Philistine, with his shield bearer in front of him, kept coming closer to David. He looked David over and saw that he was only a boy, ruddy and handsome, and he despised him. He said to David, "Am I a dog, that you come at me with sticks?" And the Philistine cursed David by his gods. "Come here," he said, "and I'll give your flesh to the birds of the air and the beasts of the field!"[1]

What came out of David in the ensuing moments is, to me, even more amazing than his battlefield victory. I love his response here in the heat of the moment because it reflects what he had been doing in the relative cool of the preceding years. What came out of him now had been building for a long, long time. According to Samuel:

> David said to the Philistine, "You come against me with sword and spear and javelin, but I come against you in the name of the

> LORD Almighty, the God of the armies of Israel, whom you have defied. This day the LORD will hand you over to me, and I'll strike you down and cut off your head. Today I will give the carcasses of the Philistine army to the birds of the air and the beasts of the earth, and the whole world will know that there is a God in Israel. All those gathered here will know that it is not by sword or spear that the LORD saves; for the battle is the LORD's, and he will give all of you into our hands."[2]

This was David's lay-it-on-the-table moment. He couldn't fake it now. He responded to Goliath out of the faith that was brimming over in him, boldly asserting that he was standing there not on his own but as a proxy for the Almighty. As if he had seen it happen a thousand times before, David stated matter-of-factly what was about to happen—"The Lord will hand you over to me, and I'll strike you down and cut off your head"—to one more enemy who defied the Lord. As if he had just come from coffee with the Almighty, David announced God's desire that people the world over know there was a God in Israel. And like one who had been on the winning side of many such victories, he made it known that the battle belonged to the Lord.

The big question is, How did David know all this? Easy…from the Scriptures. All those lazy days with the sheep, all those years in obscurity, all that time that the other boys wasted on PlayStation and half-hour sitcoms, he was meditating on Scripture. Learning stories of God's miraculous intervention in the conquest of Canaan. Reflecting on accounts of God's deliverance of the people of Israel from the land of Egypt. David stored up the Word in his heart when times were good, and when times suddenly got tough, the Word came out of him in power.

The point of this chapter is to persuade you to hide the Word of God in your heart now, while you wait on the Lord for the fulfillment of your dream. The apostle Paul exhorted the church to "let the word of Christ dwell in you richly."[3] I've spent a number of years discovering this principle for myself, implementing it in my own life, and teaching its practical value, and here's what I've learned: Whatever is in you when you get in the heat of the moment is what's going to come out of you. Jesus said it this way: "The good man brings good things out of the good stored up in him, and the evil man brings evil things out of the evil stored up in him."[4] Our responses are never random. What we've stored up when times are good is what will supply our strength when the heat is on.

The Best Defense Is a Good Offense

In the previous chapter, we explored the tendency to live right next to the Enemy's camp and thus put ourselves in the position where we're always playing defense. Well, Jesus made it irrefutably clear that in dealing with the Enemy and his nefarious designs, the best defense is a good offense. By now I hope we agree that when we live passively, the appeal of the devil's work and the inclination of our own sin natures are going to make life a constant struggle. And by now I hope we've also conceded that resigning ourselves to playing defense all the time is a recipe for misery and failure. So should we conclude, then, that the whole thing is hopeless? At the end of the day, is our adversary just more powerful than we are? Should we merely hang on to the hope of heaven, cling to the promise of forgiveness through Christ, and hunker down till we slink into heaven by the skin of our teeth? To answer these questions adequately, I think I need a new subheading.

NO!

Friend, it's true that our plight in this fallen world, in this wicked and depraved generation, in this maddeningly sin-prone flesh is challenging. And it's true that our adversary is no wilting flower. But remember what Jesus said to his disciples toward the end of his life on earth: "In this world you will have trouble. But take heart! I have overcome the world."[5] And years later, after Christ had died, conquered sin and death, risen from the grave, empowered his successors, and ascended to the Father, and after the miracle of sharing in the death of Christ and sharing in his resurrection life had become clear, his best friend let on in a letter that that victory is ours as well. John wrote to the burgeoning church,

> Everyone born of God overcomes the world. This is the victory that has overcome the world, even our faith. Who is it that overcomes the world? Only he who believes that Jesus is the Son of God.[6]

Elsewhere, John punctuated this idea and erased any doubt as to where the power lies: "You, dear children, are from God and have overcome them, because *the one who is in you is greater than the one who is in the world.*"[7]

There it is, clear and unmistakable: The devil is more powerful than you, but Christ in you is more powerful than the devil. So it is your choice every time. Do you want to prevail, or do you want to get kicked around again? Do you want victory, or do you want defeat? The decision is yours.

Here this book turns into a Choose-Your-Own-Adventure. (Remember this from when we were kids? I loved them and hated them because they had a unique ability to inflame both bizarre extremes of my personality. The ADD boy in me loved the way they capitalized on, even celebrated, my impulsive whims; the borderline-neurotic engineer boy in me was then driven crazy analyzing the vast contingencies, the logically absurd theoretical possibilities, and the ceaseless opportunity costs of foraying into whatever capricious adventure ADD boy chose.)

If you want the power to come from you, turn to the end of the book and have a nice life.

If you want the power to come from Christ in you, keep reading.

IT IS WRITTEN...

Matthew 4 tells the story of Jesus's lowest point in his life so far. He had just sprung onto the public scene from a life of total obscurity, showing up at the ministry venue of his cousin John and being proclaimed "the Lamb of God"[8] by the unconventional baptizer in the hearing of everybody. The cat was out of the bag now. John made it clear to the crowd that Jesus was the one for whose arrival he had been preparing them all this time and that now "He must become greater; I must become less."[9] The dove descended on Jesus, the Father established Jesus's mandate to lead by publicly declaring love and support for him, people started following him...and then the story took a turn for the unexpected: "Jesus was led by the Spirit into the desert to be tempted by the devil."[10] Here begins the dual ministry of Jesus, redeeming us from the curse of sin and modeling for us the overcoming life.

It is important to note that in Jesus's encounter with the devil, he operated entirely from his human nature. A core tenet of our understanding of Christ is that, while on the earth, he was both fully God and fully man. Theologians call this the *hypostatic union.* As God-man, Jesus could have dealt handily with the devil, hungry or not, simply by pulling from his divine nature. The one who was with the Father at the creation of all things could have put an end to that situation in short order—just as he could have come down from the cross without any problem—but he chose not to. Preferring to complete the work his Father had assigned him and to set an example for us of how to resist the Enemy, Jesus instead unsheathed his weapon—the very same weapon you and I have at our disposal—and waged a counterattack.

The account of the conflict continues:

> After fasting forty days and forty nights, [Jesus] was hungry. The tempter came to him and said, "If you are the Son of God, tell these stones to become bread."
>
> Jesus answered, "It is written: 'Man does not live on bread alone, but on every word that comes from the mouth of God.' "
>
> Then the devil took him to the holy city and had him stand on the highest point of the temple. "If you are the Son of God," he said, "throw yourself down. For it is written:
>
> " 'He will command his angels concerning you,
> and they will lift you up in their hands,
> so that you will not strike your foot against a stone.' "
>
> Jesus answered him, "It is also written: 'Do not put the Lord your God to the test.' "
>
> Again, the devil took him to a very high mountain and

> showed him all the kingdoms of the world and their splendor. "All this I will give you," he said, "if you will bow down and worship me."
>
> Jesus said to him, "Away from me, Satan! For it is written: 'Worship the Lord your God, and serve him only.' "
>
> Then the devil left him, and angels came and attended him.[11]

Jesus did not engage the Enemy by (1) saying, "Enough of you, Satan!" and striking him down or remanding him to the underworld, which he certainly could have done with the God-power at his disposal; or (2) arguing, debating, calling his accountability partner, or employing any other faculty or tactic of his human nature. Three times the devil came at Jesus with the full force of his power, and each time Jesus responded only with these three words: It is written. Jesus showed us how to wield the most potent weapon in the heavenly arsenal. Functioning as a human, he showed us humans how to tap into the power of God, how to harness and leverage the reality that the one in us is greater than the one in the world.

What was in Jesus is what came out of him. He didn't have time to look up passages in a concordance or call his mom to ask where that verse in Deuteronomy was that talked about testing God. Come on, you know it's true. In the heat of the moment, when the devil is in your chops, it's like Luke and Wedge flying down the trench on the surface of the Death Star trying to fire a proton torpedo and hit the thermal exhaust port: You only get one shot. If you miss or you don't pull the trigger, it's all over. It's nice to think that when you're in that moment, standing face to face with the full fury of hell, you'll call your accountability partner—but you know full well that is not going to happen.

How to Blow Up the Death Star (and How Not To)

There are two reasons we lose when we try to destroy the Death Star: (1) We try to fire energy beams when we've been instructed that only proton torpedoes will work, and (2) we botch it up and fail to fire because we haven't become a skilled enough X-wing pilot to get the shot off. Now, it's true, the Death Star is large and ominous and powerful and occupied by sinister-looking people with British accents, but we all know it can be destroyed. What it takes, though, is knowing which armament will work and having been well trained long before getting in the heat of the moment.

Jesus massacred the devil that day in the wilderness, and just to show it could be done, he did it in the weakest human condition imaginable. What was Jesus's secret? He fired the right weapon, and he had trained up in its use. Having long since become convinced that God's Word is "living and active" and "sharper than any double-edged sword,"[12] Jesus had devoted himself during the preceding thirty years of relative calm and obscurity to getting the Word to dwell in him richly. As a young man, long before his ministry calling came to fruition, he was poring over God's Word, storing it away inside him. At an age when other boys were teasing the girls and skipping rocks in the pond, Jesus was "in the temple courts, sitting among the teachers, listening to them and asking them questions."[13] Like the psalmist of old, Jesus might have said, "I have hidden your word in my heart that I might not sin against you."[14] And, indeed, when the moment of trial came—and it will come to all of us—what was hidden in him came out of him and enabled him to defeat the Enemy and not sin against the Lord.

WHAT ARE YOU DOING WITH THE WORD?

I love the beginning of Proverbs 7:

> My son, keep my words
> and store up my commands within you...
> guard my teachings as the apple of your eye.
> Bind them on your fingers;
> write them on the tablet of your heart.[15]

Four ideas here are important to our understanding the principle of this chapter:

1. "Store up my commands within you." If you finish this chapter, put the book down, and walk away thinking that I'm only saying you need to read your Bible, then you've missed the point and I've failed at my assignment. Now before I proceed with this explanation, let me clarify that you should, in fact, read your Bible. It is the one indispensable guide to life; it is full of useful, practical instruction on how to live effectively; and it is the one authorized biography of God. It is important for every Christian to read his or her Bible. But that is not the point I'm making here.

To employ the Word as a weapon—to benefit from its full evil-crushing potency—we have to do more with it than merely read a few verses in the morning, check the box in our Bible-reading guide, and get a star on our Sunday-school chart. That's like buying a Ferrari and only driving it across town to the grocery store and back at thirty-five miles an hour. Sure, you get some benefit from it. You get where you need to go a lot faster than walking, and you ride in a really cool car. But you never experience what that machine can really do, what it was designed to do. You get some benefit, but you don't get the *full* benefit.

To harness the full power of the Word of God and see the devil flee like a squealing schoolgirl when we get in the heat of the moment, we have to store it up in our hearts. It's like preparing for financial low points in our lives: We store up extra money so we don't crash on the rocks when things take a downward turn. In the same way, store up the Word inside you. Pore over it, memorize large chunks of it, and have it locked and loaded in the ammunition chamber of your mind. Then, when the roaring lion pounces and seeks to devour you, all you have to do is all you have time to do—pull the trigger.

2. "Guard my teachings as the apple of your eye." This is an odd cliché—the apple of one's eye. I generally know what it means from its usage, but as I was writing this I became intrigued as to how it came about, so I decided to research it. Here's what I learned:

> The phrase means "That which one holds dearest," as in "You're the apple of my eye." Its origin is the Bible (Deut. 32:10), which says the Lord kept Israel "as the apple of his eye." "Pupillam," or pupil, is actually the Latin for the "apple" of the phrase, but English translation[s] of the Bible used "apple" because this was the early word for the pupil of the eye, which was thought to be a solid apple-shaped body. Because it is so essential to sight, the eye's apple, or pupil, is to be cherished and protected and "the apple of one's eye" came to mean anything extremely precious. The literal translation of the Hebrew phrase, incidentally, is "You are as the little man in the eye" (one's own reflection in the pupil of another's eye).[16]

So the lesson here is to treat the Scripture like the little man in the eye. Just kidding. But the idea is clear, however bizarre the term may be. The apple of your eye is the thing that delights you most, what holds first position in your heart.

I have a three-year-old daughter named Ellie, and she is the apple of my eye. A lot of people make me light up (chief among them my wife, Mauri), several activities energize me, (like mountain biking), and numerous places have captured my heart (such as the Serengeti), but Ellie is unique in her capacity to flip the switch of delight inside me, melt my heart, and get me to do anything she wants. In truth, she has me wrapped around her inch-and-a-half finger. She possesses some sway over me like the Jedi mind trick that Obi-Wan used on the Storm Troopers:

OBI-WAN: "You don't need to see his identification."

STORM TROOPERS: "We don't need to see his identification."

OBI-WAN: (Waving his hand slowly in front of the Storm Troopers) "These aren't the droids you're looking for."

STORM TROOPERS: "These aren't the droids we're looking for."

The idea here is to make the Word of God the apple of your eye. Regardless of how you feel or what your sinful nature desires, stage a coup d'état, overpower the ruling regime, and forcefully put the Scriptures on the throne of your heart. Make it your single greatest source of delight. Choose to cherish the eternal Truth of God.

We all have an apple of our eye, whether we realize it or not. Every one of us has something—some group or pastime or set of ideas or whatever—that holds the keys to our hearts. All of us have something that whispers to our hearts more clearly than anything else and informs its inclinations. Very often you can tell what sits on the throne of people's hearts by what comes out of them most fluently. Some people spew

Seinfeld episodes in their entirety. Others wear their political dogma on their sleeves. (I have a friend who is an atheist and a brazen liberal. For him, everything is about homosexuality and the vast right-wing conspiracy.) Still others retain vast reservoirs of useless *Star Wars* trivia that trickle out at the most random moments. Um...yeah.

But staging a coup to overthrow sin is not enough. The exhortation goes beyond making the choice to put God's Word in the Oval Office of our hearts. If we are to cultivate the full power of the Word in our lives, we must not stop at making the Word our heart's chief delight; we must *guard* it as such. Knowing that our hearts tend to wander in search of momentary gratification requires us to be vigilant in defending the Word's ascension in our hearts and solidifying its rule. We have to fortify the palace of our hearts lest another strongman wage a counter-insurgency, trump our coup d'état, and topple the newly established regime before the new business cards are even back from the printer. So how do we put the Word on the throne and then guard it as our hearts' first delight? Read on!

3. "Bind them on your fingers." Remember Uncle Billy in *It's a Wonderful Life*? He always had strings tied around his fingers to remind him to do this or that. Tragically, the one that was supposed to remind him to deposit the eight grand didn't do its job, and George just about came to a watery demise. Nonetheless, the purpose of Uncle Billy's tying strings around his fingers was to keep some things on his radar screen, to maintain certain priorities at the forefront of his mind. In the same way, bind the words of the Scripture on your fingers. Take deliberate, even apparently senseless action to get the resistance movement into power and then keep the new regime stably in place.

I coach young men of God to do this all the time. One of their most common protestations is, "But I don't feel it. How can I make it first in my heart?" I always tell them two things. Here's how the conversation goes:

"First, if you don't feel it, fake it," I say. "Act like someone who genuinely feels a burning love for the Word of God. Do the things that someone who cherishes the Word would do."

"But isn't that being—*gasp!*—inauthentic?" my friend replies.

(I love messing with homogenized postmodern thinking! You know, I've found that there are fewer truly postmodern people than society is duped into thinking there are. A lot of people are just consumers of postmodernism. They buy postmodernism in a juice box, and they buy it in bulk at Wal-Mart.)

Then I say, "I suppose you could look at it that way. And you would be forced to conclude, by the same logic, that when a husband no longer feels burning passion for his wife or a desire to spend time with his loud, energetic children, it would be inauthentic for him to go home to them. To be truly 'authentic,' he really needs to leave his wife and kids, buy a sports car, and meet somebody new on the Internet with whom he really connects. The problem is, this is foolishness. He would be destroying his life and the lives of the people who are most beloved to him and whose care and well-being their Creator has entrusted to him. But, hey, it would be authentic."

Usually it's quiet at this point in the conversation. Then I continue:

"If you consider authenticity to be following your heart on whatever whim it leads you, you are an idiot. The Bible makes it plain: 'The heart is deceitful above all things and beyond cure.'[17] Your heart is not to be followed; it is to be subdued. David repeatedly told his heart what to do. When he was feeling down, he interrogated it, 'Why are you downcast, O my soul? Why so disturbed within me?' Then he instructed it, 'Put your hope in God, for I will yet praise him.'[18] A fool follows his feelings; a wise man chooses his convictions."

Still reeling a bit from the sudden realization of just how frail his flaky postmodernism is, my young friend usually moves the conversation on:

"That makes sense. So what do I do with the fact that what's on the throne of my heart is not what my heart really wants?"

"That's the second thing I was going to tell you," I respond. "John Bevere presents an idea in his book *Drawing Near* that is valuable here. He says that you hunger for what you feed on. And it's true. If your diet consists mainly of Big Bacon Classics, a wild mixed-field-greens salad is not going to appeal to you. You're going to crave Big Bacon Classics. But if you choose to change your diet—even if you have to hold your nose and gag it down—eventually you'll find that you don't crave Big Bacon Classics anymore. In fact, they make you feel heavy and greasy and gross when you eat them, and now they aren't appealing at all. You find yourself, instead, ordering wild mixed-field-greens salads. I can tell you; it's true. I made it through college on pizza and Big Borderitos, but then I married somewhat of a health nut. Well, when you're married, if you want things to go well for you, you eat what is prepared for dinner. So I started eating salads and steamed vegetables and hormone-free meats, and now, guess what? When I'm out of town eating in a restaurant half a country away from my house, where I could order the unhealthiest things on the menu and my wife would never know, I choose healthy stuff. It's what I crave now."

The response is often something like, "Bro, that'll never happen to me!"

To which I reply, "Oh, you just wait and see!"

Our hearts operate the same way. If we feed on *Seinfeld* reruns, that's what we're going to hunger for. Put the Word on the throne of your heart, and your heart's not going to like it at first. But remember, we choose our convictions. So forcibly change your diet and feed on the Scriptures. Instruct your soul—as David did—to consume the Word of God rather than junk food, and watch your appetite change over time.

4. "Write them on the tablet of your heart." People with a lot of tattoos are interesting to me. They have chosen to consider their skin a canvas—a tablet, if you will—on which they have someone etch indelible messages about themselves to the world. Anytime you meet tattoo people, that's what you remember about them. One may be a brilliant microbiologist, another an opera singer, and another a sword juggler, but what will stick in people's minds is lots of tattoos.

Pastor Ted has long taught our congregation not merely to read the Word but to consume it. Ingest it. Get it in you so it starts mixing up your DNA and, after a while, defines you. Like tattoos, it's what people will see and remember about you.

The command to inscribe the Word of God "on the tablet of your heart" establishes the fact that our hearts are tablets. They are imminently markable; in fact, they are made for inscription. Let me suggest four ways you can start inscribing.

1. Soak in the Word. I have a copy of the entire Bible on CD, narrated by James Earl Jones. (It's fantastic—just imagine Darth Vader's voice piercing the barrier of eternity and terrifying all the people getting baptized, saying, "This is my Son, in whom I am well pleased." You half expect him to continue, "Luke, I am your father.") I have the CD playing first thing in the morning when I wake up and get into the shower. As I'm clearing my head for the day, the first thoughts entering my mind are the Scriptures. I also play the CD in my car when I'm driving to work and around town. At any opportunity, I choose to soak in the Word, and I find that increasingly I hunger for it.

2. Pray the Word. In my prayer times, I almost always pray through the ideas from a passage in the Bible. The easiest place to start is the book of Psalms. For example, you might pray Psalm 103 like this: *My soul praises you, O Lord; with all my inmost being, I praise your holy name. Lord, thank you for all your benefits—you forgive all my sins and heal all my diseases, you redeem my life from the pit and crown me with love and compassion, you satisfy my desires with good things so that my youth is renewed like the eagle's. Lord, you work righteousness and justice for all the oppressed. Make known your ways to me like you did to Moses, and your deeds like you did to the people of Israel.* It's easy, really—mainly it's changing a lot of third-person pronouns to second-person pronouns on the fly as you read the Bible aloud—and it's incredibly powerful.

3. Meditate on the Word. After Moses died, God spoke to Joshua to prepare him for leading the people of Israel. One of God's instructions to Joshua was, "Do not let this Book of the Law depart from your mouth; meditate on it day and night, so that you may be careful to do everything written in it. Then you will be prosperous and successful."[19] Meditating on the Word can sound scary and foreboding—I imagine monks in brown robes chanting in a monotone voice as they meditate on Holy Writ—but it really is just another matter of disciplining our thoughts. Meditating is simply continuing to ponder and reflect throughout the day on the Scripture you read this morning when you were sitting on the sofa in your sweat pants with a cup of coffee. I think of it like marinating a steak. You don't just dip the sirloin tips into the teriyaki sauce and then throw them on the grill; you have to let them get saturated so the flavor really sets in. The scripture passage might as well read, "Be careful not to read the Bible just to check the box and have it go in one ear and out the other. Be deliberate to continue thinking about it, and let it soak in."

4. Dig into the Word. It's as easy as a paperback Bible and a ballpoint pen. (Say that out loud. It has great rhythm, kind of like "two turntables and a microphone.") I know, you love to carry and read from the expensive, leather-covered Bible with your name embossed in gold on the front and the wafer-thin pages, but put that one on display somewhere for a while. Instead, go buy a five-dollar paperback Bible with normal-weight-paper pages and enough margin that's not consumed with a Bible scholar's thoughts so that you can make some notes of your own in it and start using that as your primary study Bible. Now, put the three-dollar, liquid-ink rollerball pen in your desk drawer and get a thirty-cent Bic ballpoint. Some people also find a highlighter or colored pencils to be helpful. Okay, now you're ready. Always study the Bible with a pen in hand, and underline or highlight the ideas that stand out to you. Then, when you've finished reading the passage, go back and meditate on the portions you underlined. Write notes in the margin about the things that come to you. Then, when you're finished meditating, pray through the marked passages.

The symbol of this whole idea for me is my college Bible. It's a paperback copy I received free at a student missions conference early in my college career (or, rather, it was a paperback copy—now it's all held together with cardboard and duct tape). I brought it home from that trip and started studying in it because I wasn't as hesitant about marking it up as I was about marking up the nice leather-bound copy my mom and dad had given me. As I prayed about being a pastor during those years, the Lord showed me that it was time, right then, to start learning the Word the way a pastor should know it. As I said earlier, a name on a door or a title on a business card or a paycheck from a church does not make you a pastor. All the titles and positions are just people's ratification of what

God has already done inside me. It's what's in me that determines what comes out of me, and it's what comes out of me that made me a pastor long before I ever heard of New Life Church.

By the end of four years of college, my ragged old Bible was marked on nearly every page, packed with insights from a thousand light bulbs that went on during a thousand quiet times of various shapes and sizes through the years. Now, all these years later, I can look back through all the twists and turns along the unlikely path that has led to my ministry and point to that Bible, and all that it testifies to, as the secret source of it all.

Chapter 13

The Secret of the Secret Place

Thou hast formed us for Thyself, and our hearts are restless till they find rest in Thee.... Let me die, lest I die, if only I may see Thy face.

—ST. AUGUSTINE OF HIPPO

Victory or defeat is your choice. The prescription for success has already been written. You decide whether to follow it. In the last chapter, we started considering where we get the power to go on the attack, to play our game rather than the Enemy's. There are two sources of power in this world, two access points to the realm of God, like phone booths in and out of the Matrix, like wall outlets for the ready-and-waiting current of supernatural power. One is the Word of God—that was the subject of the last chapter—and the other is the intimate friendship of God.

The premise of this chapter is that God dispenses his power in greater measure on behalf of his friends than on behalf of other more distant acquaintances, and that is off-putting for some people. The very idea that God has friends—some individuals among the world he loves whom, for some reason, he especially *likes*—can be disquieting because it imposes a measure of subjectivity onto a God whom many would prefer to be objective. Uncomfortable though it may be, this notion is irrefutable in Scripture. King Jehoshaphat prayed, "O our God, did you not drive out the inhabitants of this land before your people Israel and give it forever to the descendants of Abraham *your friend?*"[1] Joseph, Moses, Daniel, and many others seemed to enjoy not only the love of God their Creator but the fellowship of God their friend.

This was also true for David. Let's go back to his life.

Have you ever noticed that at the beginning of some of the psalms David wrote, there are notes that give historical or geographical context? Psalm 63 is one of these. Its preamble reads, "A psalm of David. When he was in the Desert of Judah." That tidbit is unexciting until you consider the circumstances—what David was doing in the desert—and the substance of the text—what he was writing while he was in the desert. Take these together, and you find a gem.

To begin, we ought to look at what David was doing in the desert. After killing Goliath, he quickly became the toast of the town. All Israel was celebrating him. The king, too, recognized his abilities: "Whatever Saul sent him to do, David did it so successfully that Saul gave him a high rank in the army. This pleased all the people, and Saul's officers as well."[2] David had stayed steady during the agonizing season of sameness that followed the prophet's visit. He had learned to submit to God's delegated authority, served humbly, and faithfully done the work along the way. Now he was working at the highest levels of government, and everybody knew his name. His calling was unfolding perfectly.

A Hundred Foreskins Spell the Inevitable

Things were great for a while. David was finally ascending to greatness, the people favored him, and Saul was happy. After a while, though, the folks around the palace started noticing a subtle shift in the social climate of the king's world. David's successes multiplied and—slowly at first, then steadily—this inflamed the fragile king and his ultrafragile ego:

> When the men were returning home after David had killed the Philistine, the women came out from all the towns of Israel to meet King Saul with singing and dancing, with joyful songs and with tambourines and lutes. As they danced, they sang:
>
> "Saul has slain his thousands,
> and David his tens of thousands."
>
> Saul was very angry; this refrain galled him. "They have credited David with tens of thousands," he thought, "but me with

> only thousands. What more can he get but the kingdom?" And from that time on Saul kept a jealous eye on David.[3]

Once his heart darkened, it wasn't long before Saul was looking for ways to set David up for failure. When it came out that Saul's daughter Michal was in love with David, the king was pleased. "'I will give her to him,' he thought, 'so that she may be a snare to him and so that the hand of the Philistines may be against him.'"[4] Soon Saul's jealousy bubbled over, and his plotting took a turn for the sinister. To David's humble protestation that he was unworthy of the king's daughter, the neurotic ruler replied, "The king wants no other price for the bride than a hundred Philistine foreskins, to take revenge on his enemies." Scripture adds the intent of Saul's nefarious scheme "was to have David fall by the hands of the Philistines."[5] Finally, the king's resentment and jealousy deteriorated into abject loathing, and "Saul...remained [David's] enemy the rest of his days."[6]

From this point on, Saul was determined to kill David at any cost. In the face of such powerful and targeted adversity, our hero did what any sensible man would do: He ran. Saul frenetically pursued David from one city to the next, the younger man each time barely escaping. When finally the monarch let up pursuit to tend to matters on the home front, the beleaguered and bewildered shepherd-king was able to seek out a suitable hiding place, "and David went...and lived in the strongholds of En Gedi."[7]

The First Night in En Gedi

Now it was official. Until this point, David had been running, evading, playing out the twisted game in which he had found himself, barely able to catch his breath. But now that he had time to stop and think about what was happening, the bitter reality came crashing in fast and sudden like a tsunami, and his dreams that had just started to peek all timid and hopeful out of their shell were dashed on the hard, sandy shoal. He was in exile. The throne had been so close he could taste it, and now it was a million miles away. For the foreseeable future, the wilderness was his home.

Imagine that first night in En Gedi. For the moment anyway, the pressure is off. Nobody's chasing you. At last your defenses can stand down. Now there is time to think. Now—like Jason Bourne after he ran and fought and got shot at and shot back and killed people with his bare hands and had a high-speed car chase and got away, and then, finally, got alone and sat down to process the crushing reality that he had lost everything and didn't know who he was—you realize all at once that what you had is gone, and you are all alone. It must have been as David was lying there in a cave trying to go to sleep that first night—tired, cold, hungry, lonely, and scared—that he hit rock bottom.

The place David chose to hide out was En Gedi. According to the *New Bible Dictionary,* En Gedi was an "important oasis and fresh water spring west of the Dead Sea, allotted to Judah at the conquest. David hid there, its rugged terrain and fertility making it an ideal refuge."[8] It was an oasis. An island of fertility in the middle of a desert. In Judah. And it was here—at En Gedi—that David penned Psalm 63:

> O God, you are my God,
>   earnestly I seek you;
> my soul thirsts for you,
>   my body longs for you,
> in a dry and weary land
>   where there is no water.

I have seen you in the sanctuary
and beheld your power and your glory.
Because your love is better than life,
my lips will glorify you.
I will praise you as long as I live,
and in your name I will lift up my hands.
My soul will be satisfied as with the richest of foods;
with singing lips my mouth will praise you.

On my bed I remember you;
I think of you through the watches of the night.
Because you are my help,
I sing in the shadow of your wings.
My soul clings to you;
your right hand upholds me.[9]

In my view, the first eight verses of Psalm 63 are the most poignant, exquisite expression of a person's desire for the intimate fellowship of the Almighty in the entire Bible. Distressed, calm, at leisure, or otherwise, no person in any circumstance ever penned more passionate words of love for the Creator of his soul. How much more striking, then, to think that David was in the crisis of his life, likely feeling the worst he had ever felt, and these are the words that came out of him!

As we discussed in the last chapter, whatever is in you is going to come out of you when the heat is on. That's what happened here. David didn't start doggedly desiring God's intimate presence there at En Gedi. What came out of him when he hit rock bottom reflected what he had stored up in his heart over the course of a lifetime. You can imagine

David the teenage shepherd boy lying in the pasture on a slow summer afternoon, writing at he watched the sheep:

> The LORD is my shepherd, I shall not be in want.
> He makes me lie down in green pastures,
> he leads me beside quiet waters,
> he restores my soul.
> He guides me in paths of righteousness
> for his name's sake.
> Even though I walk
> through the valley of the shadow of death,
> I will fear no evil,
> for you are with me;
> your rod and your staff,
> they comfort me.
>
> You prepare a table before me
> in the presence of my enemies.
> You anoint my head with oil;
> my cup overflows.
> Surely goodness and love will follow me
> all the days of my life,
> and I will dwell in the house of the LORD
> forever.[10]

While the other boys' minds wandered to a game or a girl, thoughts of intimate walks alone with the God of his forefathers preoccupied David's mind. The abundance of written material we have from David's pen makes it clear that he spent a disproportionate amount of his time thinking about, dreaming of, hungering for the presence of God. Then when he lies down one night, collects his thoughts, and realizes he is at his life's lowest point, where else would he go? What else would come out of him?

Why God Liked David So Much

David's desire to "dwell in the house of the LORD forever" echoes throughout his writing. "The house of the LORD"—a metaphor for the intimate presence of God—emerges as a favorite motif of David's. In Psalm 26:8, he declared, "I love the house where you live, O LORD, the place where your glory dwells." My favorite is Psalm 27:4:

> One thing I ask of the LORD,
>   this is what I seek:
> that I may dwell in the house of the LORD
>   all the days of my life,
> to gaze upon the beauty of the LORD
>   and to seek him in his temple.

David was not expressing his preference to spend his life in the tabernacle; what he wanted was to know God the way he had heard that the men of old knew God. Adam walked with God in the garden in the cool of the day. Abraham was called the friend of God. Moses spoke with God face to face. David knew all this, and he wanted it. To be sure, he fully understood God had established laws to appropriate the covenant and set apart his people. He knew about temple worship and the sacrifices and the fellowship offerings. He knew how to keep all those laws, and still he wanted more. Over time, resolve steels into determination, and David's resolve was plain and unmistakable: "In righteousness I will see your face; when I awake, I will be satisfied with seeing your likeness."[11]

Incidentally, this is why God chose David to be king. It's true that Saul had disobeyed God and sinned and that God was looking for a replacement king. But David sinned too. So did Solomon. So did Moses, Elijah, and all the other great leaders. What motivated God to oust Saul was the king's evident disregard for the Almighty. Saul wanted the stuff of God and loved the work of God, but he seemed indifferent to God himself. After Saul's disobedience, the prophet Samuel delivered a stinging message: "Now your kingdom will not endure; the LORD has sought out a man after his own heart and appointed him leader of his people."[12] God wanted David not for his skill or his wealth or his network. David's appeal wasn't his résumé; it was his insatiable desire for the presence of the Almighty.

This may have been why David always got out of the jams he landed in. Whoever the assailant, wherever the battle, however outnumbered David was—whatever the astronomically perilous situation—God always delivered him. Reading through David's life, you get the impression that he was like a comic-book hero. There was always drama, he was perpetually against the ropes, and he invariably came through unscathed. It's tempting for us to read David's story and marginalize this phenomenon by presuming that he had the favor-of-God pixie dust sprinkled on him at birth or the protection wand waved over him, but it's just not true. If his vast writings establish anything with certainty, it's that David was just like you and me. He experienced all the same emotions, he struggled the same way through hardship, and he made some of the same blunders we do. No, David didn't get out of a jam because of some birthright; he got out because God really liked him.

In Psalm 18—which, according to the note at the beginning, David sang "when the LORD delivered him from the hand of all his enemies and from the hand of Saul"—David recounted the drama and peril of his plight of many years:

The cords of death entangled me;
the torrents of destruction overwhelmed me.
The cords of the grave coiled around me;
the snares of death confronted me.[13]

Equally dramatic was the elaborate rescue mission he described next:

In my distress I called to the LORD;
I cried to my God for help.
From his temple he heard my voice;
my cry came before him, into his ears.
The earth trembled and quaked,
and the foundations of the mountains shook;
they trembled because he was angry.
Smoke rose from his nostrils;
consuming fire came from his mouth,
burning coals blazed out of it.
He parted the heavens and came down;
dark clouds were under his feet.
He mounted the cherubim and flew;
he soared on the wings of the wind.

He made darkness his covering, his canopy around him—
the dark rain clouds of the sky.
Out of the brightness of his presence clouds advanced,
with hailstones and bolts of lightning.
The LORD thundered from heaven;
the voice of the Most High resounded.
He shot his arrows and scattered the enemies,
great bolts of lightning and routed them.
The valleys of the sea were exposed
and the foundations of the earth laid bare
at your rebuke, O LORD,
at the blast of breath from your nostrils.

He reached down from on high and took hold of me;
he drew me out of deep waters.
He rescued me from my powerful enemy,
from my foes, who were too strong for me.
They confronted me in the day of my disaster,
but the LORD was my support.[14]

I especially enjoy the image of God's saddling up one of the cherubim, flying down to the earth, and personally defeating David's foe. But to those of us who have been beaten down, kicked around, and left for dead, this image is a pipe dream. You get discouraged, thinking this would never happen for you, and you are just about to close the Bible and put it back on the shelf when your eye stops at the next verse: "He brought me out into a spacious place; he rescued me because he delighted in me."[15] Then it all makes sense. God's deliverance wasn't arbitrary, and it wasn't favoritism. God delivered David because he liked him so much, and he liked him so much because, day after day, year after year, tirelessly, reliably, relentlessly, David sought the presence of the Lord.

"You Have Heard It Said..."

Jesus upended many religious paradigms during his time on the earth, none more radically than the idea of how we should relate to God. Jesus taught and modeled the revolutionary notion that we can access spiritual power through personal friendship with the Father. Overturning the presumption that close fellowship with the Almighty was the exclusive domain of a chosen handful, Jesus made it clear that intimate fellowship with God is accessible to everyone. No longer is the power of God reserved for the elite and enlightened; Jesus brought the overpowering concept of divine friendship down to the level of everyman.

Jesus had a habit of turning religious convention on its head. Nowhere is this more evident than in the series of teachings recorded in Matthew 5–7. Over and over, Jesus pounded this one theme: "You have heard that it was said... But I tell you..." Challenging religious norms of the day, he established a new code of righteousness through these teachings that served as the foundational ideology for his ministry. The implication is that the religious leaders and teachers of the Law had over time built a sort of scaffolding around the Law, persuaded the people to treat the additional rules as indistinguishable from the Torah, and used the product for their own manipulative, prideful ends. In response to these manmade teachings, Jesus overturned the ideological tables in his coming-out party, which scholars now call the Sermon on the Mount. His thesis statement might be Matthew 5:20: "For I tell you that unless your righteousness surpasses that of the Pharisees and the teachers of the law, you will certainly not enter the kingdom of heaven."

Then he began:

> You have heard that it was said to the people long ago, "Do not murder, and anyone who murders will be subject to judgment." But I tell you that anyone who is angry with his brother will be subject to judgment....
>
> You have heard that it was said, "Do not commit adultery." But I tell you that anyone who looks at a woman lustfully has already committed adultery with her in his heart....
>
> You have heard that it was said, "Eye for eye, and tooth for tooth." But I tell you, Do not resist an evil person. If someone strikes you on the right cheek, turn to him the other also....
>
> You have heard that it was said, "Love your neighbor and hate your enemy." But I tell you: Love your enemies and pray for those who persecute you.[16]

This series of contrasting conceptions of righteousness set the stage for a curious curve ball. Jesus continued his message this way:

> And when you pray, do not be like the hypocrites, for they love to pray standing in the synagogues and on the street corners to be seen by men. I tell you the truth, they have received their reward in full. But when you pray, go into your room, close the door and pray to your Father, who is unseen. Then your Father, who sees what is done in secret, will reward you.[17]

The inference here is astounding. Jesus was saying that there is a format for finding God, a setting by which he is—and one by which he is not—accessible through prayer. The fact that the hypocrites who pray in public have already received their reward implies that nothing more can be found by seeking God their way. By seeking God another way, though, there is reward to be gained. There is power to be appropriated. God's intimate presence can surely be found, but it must be sought, as it were, in secret.

There is more than that, though. Not only *can* we have intimate fellowship with the Father, Jesus taught, but we *must.* This is the perfect fulfillment of the better righteousness he had been teaching—not just to know *about* God, but to *know* God, himself, personally. At the end of his life on earth, Jesus prayed that his followers "may be one, as You, Father, are in Me, and I in You; that they also may be one in Us."[18] The very intimacy that God the Son shares with God the Father—two separate beings who are one in nature and substance—is the standard Jesus sets for our relationship with the Father. No longer, Christ seemed to say, do we need to wallow in the outer courts. Jesus came to rend the temple curtain and let us into the inner chamber. Jesus came to give us unfettered, full-time access to him who, for centuries past, none but the chosen few knew—and they knew him only in part, from a distance, and in small, measured doses. And now that we have the access, staying in the outer court is no longer an option.

Climbing the Wrong Ladder

The greatest tragedy ever is missing the one who made us and thereby missing the first purpose for which we were made. "Not everyone who says to Me, 'Lord, Lord,'" went Jesus's troubling words later in his sermon, "shall enter the kingdom of heaven, but he who does the will of My Father in heaven."[19] Okay, so saying the words isn't enough. We have to do God's will. Fair enough. But what is his will? How do we know if we're doing it? What keeps us from thinking we're doing his will all along, only to get to judgment day and receive the shock of our lives? Jesus seemed to acknowledge the possibility, adding, "Many will say to Me in that day, 'Lord, Lord, have we not prophesied in Your name, cast out demons in Your name, and done many wonders in Your name?' "[20]

In his writing Stephen Covey paints a word picture of a man climbing a ladder. He describes the painstaking ascent—sweating, sacrificing, staying focused, steadily climbing, keeping the top ever in sight, persevering through years and decades—and the subsequent deflation and emptiness of getting to the top of the ladder only to realize it was leaning on the wrong wall. The potential for this happening is completely unsatisfactory to me—and, thankfully, it is completely unnecessary. Jesus gave us the answer: "And then I will declare to them, 'I never knew you; depart from Me.' "[21] The problem was never the accuracy of the prophecies given in his name, the quality of the deliverance done in his name, or the greatness of the wonders performed in his name. The reason Jesus tells the many that he will send them away is "I never *knew* you." They spent their lives climbing a ladder only to find out when they reached the top that it had been leaning on the wrong wall.

THE SECRET OF THE SECRET PLACE

The *New King James Version* of the Bible sheds additional light on the subject with this rendering of Matthew 6: "Go into your room, and when you have shut your door, pray to your Father who is in the *secret place*."[22] The meaning, of course, is the same as in other versions, but the metaphor here highlights an important prerequisite for knowing God. There is a "place," entirely different from where we live day to day, where

God's presence can be found. This is the secret David discovered long before he ever sat on the throne: the secret of the secret place.

Jesus punctuated this idea toward the end of his sermon, exhorting his followers to "ask, and it will be given to you; seek, and you will find; knock, and it will be opened to you. For everyone who asks receives, and he who seeks finds, and to him who knocks it will be opened."[23] The point is that no magic words or power pellets or special status can get us into God's presence and favor. But there is a path that diverges from our path of least resistance, and we must seek it. There is a door that leads to a great, wonderful, unknown world, and we must knock on it. On the one hand, no one is going to overtake our faculties and force us down that path or through that door, but on the other hand, no one who goes that way will ever be denied.

One of my earliest and most vivid childhood memories is creeping downstairs at the crack of dawn (I cannot for the life of me figure out why the great revelation that occurs to teenagers concerning the high value of sleep, especially in the morning, does not even enter the minds of small children), entering the kitchen, and hearing whispers and what sounded like gentle groans coming from the family room. My childish curiosity piqued, I peered stealthily around the corner. What I saw startled me. There was my mother, down on her knees, her body draped over the ottoman, her face buried in her hands. My impulse was to rush to her side, to find out if she was hurt, but something stayed me. Instead of rushing into the room, I watched, silent, intrigued. Then I heard it again. She would intermittently whisper and groan ever so gently. *Dear God,* I remember thinking, *I wonder if she's been shot!* Then I reasoned, *Of course she hasn't been shot. We would have heard gunfire, and there would be a pool of blood.* But I couldn't get rid of the sense of dread for a while. *Maybe she had an organ fail, or she fell victim to some rare, food-borne parasite, or she was mauled by our cat and left limp and powerless. O Lord, what should I do?* After standing there paralyzed a little while longer, wondering about my mom's general health, I heard her say the most interesting thing: my name. Then my sister's, then my dad's, then my grandparents', aunts', uncles', and cousins'. *What on earth is she doing?* I thought. Then all at once it hit me: *She's...praying.* You have to understand, at that stage in my life, praying happened before meals and before bed, and it was somewhat rote. What my mom was doing was totally different. It was as if she were...with someone. As if there were another person at whose feet she joyfully knelt. I crept back upstairs, aware even at my young age that this was a moment not to disturb. That image was burned into my mind.

As long as I have known her, my mom has had her secret place. It was never one particular space—it could be the family room or the kitchen or her bedroom or wherever, as far as I knew—nor was it exactly a set amount of time. Sometimes its outward expression lasted for a long time; other times it happened in stolen moments. But she always seemed to possess a certainty about the things of God, as if she *knew* him or something. Never high-minded or holier-than-thou, my mom exuded instead a quiet confidence in what God would do. That—the quiet confidence my mom had in her relationship with God—more than any other single factor, is what drew me to my own faith in Christ as a young man.

Living in the Shadow of God

Psalm 91 adds insight to the idea of the secret place, declaring that "he who dwells in the secret place of the Most High shall abide under the shadow of the Almighty."[24] It's a good way of putting it, if you think about it. People like that—my mom, David, the ones who seemed to know something more, whom God really seemed to *like*—come off as if they live in the shadow of God. Like a little brother living in the shadow of his tough and fearless older sibling, with whom a bully would be picking a fight if he came after the smaller boy. Like a senior-ranking senator getting an office in the shadow of the Capitol because he's so important to what happens there every day that he needs to be as close as possible. David lived in the shadow of God, and that proximity enabled him to live into the dreams he had been given.

I'm going to show you four blueprints for the secret place, all from the first verse of Psalm 91.

1. The secret place is nontransferable. Part of the reason I moved to Colorado was because I love to ski. Every year, from the time I arrived until my life was overrun and forcefully taken from me by my children, I purchased a season pass at one of the area ski resorts. I remember the time a friend came to visit from out of state. I wanted to take him skiing and borrowed my local buddy's season pass so my out-of-town friend wouldn't have to buy a ticket. (Okay, so I recognize now that this wasn't the best idea—for many reasons.) Our first time through the lift line, the Australian girl (who was working for peanuts scanning tickets in the chairlift line and waiting tables at night at an overpriced Breckenridge restaurant so she could spend a year being a ski bum) zapped my pass with the gun. The gun beeped, and I skied on up to the chair. Next, she went to zap my friend's pass, looked at the picture, looked at him, looked back at the picture, and then looked at him once more, her face now covered with a cynical sort of "Do you think I'm stupid?" look: "Uh... sir...season passes are nontransferable." One person, one pass.

Notice that the Scripture reads, "*He* who dwells in the secret place." It's tempting for us to go through our lives with Christ thinking we can delegate the secret place to someone else. I've heard lots of men say things like, "All that prayin' is woman stuff. I go to work. Support the family. Pay the bills. My wife can do the deep spiritual stuff." Others say things like, "Isn't that what you get paid for, preacher?" The more spiritually savvy will spiritualize the thing and talk about how their intercessors go into the Lord's presence on their behalf. All that's fine, but it's not doing the people who are talking about it any good. Among the things Scripture clearly does not say are "He whose wife dwells..." or "He whose pastor dwells..." or "He whose intercessors dwell." Nope, the Bible is perfectly clear that the one who dwells in the secret place is the one who abides in the shadow. There is no way around it, no shortcut, and no riding on someone else's coattails. You have to go there yourself.

2. The secret place is a residence, not a rest stop. Look at the first part of the verse again: "He who *dwells* in the secret place of the most high." It's easy and gratifying to cultivate a lifestyle of stopping in and paying homage once in a while to the secret place. Often these trysts with intimacy are accompanied by extravagant shows of emotion that give an impression of great spiritual depth. Reminiscent of the Pharisees' showy praying that Jesus so harshly condemned, this sort of spirituality is actually counterproductive to our relationship with God. He does desire our intimate friendship, but he doesn't need us to throw him a bone.

God desires our full-time devotion. He intends the secret place to be our dwelling—the place where we live. Jesus told his disciples, "Remain in me, and I will remain in you. No branch can bear fruit by itself; it must remain in the vine. Neither can you bear fruit unless you remain in me."[25] Remain. Stay. Drive a spike in the ground, stake your claim, and call this place home. First Thessalonians 5:17 says, "Pray continually." Now, it's all well and good to say that, but, short of becoming a monk, how is it possible?

I spent several years languishing with a dial-up Internet connection. Remember that? It was painfully slow, you paid by the minute, and it required the dedicated use of your phone line. Consequently, you always got online, did what you had to do, and got off. Now I have a high-speed connection. Because my computer is always online, I work differently. Sometimes I'm actively sending and receiving e-mail, and other times I'm working on a Word document or balancing the checkbook. No matter what I'm doing, bytes are passing in and out of my computer. Information is always being sent and received. Like using a dial-up connection, many of us are confining our pursuit of intimacy with our heavenly Father to short, confined bursts, when he's wanting a T1 connection.

In *The Practice of the Presence of God,* a seventeenth-century monk named Brother Lawrence articulated the delight of maintaining this constant, quiet conversation with the Lord:

> I honestly cannot understand how people who claim to love the Lord can be content without practicing His presence. My preference is to retire with Him to the deepest part of my soul as often as possible. When I am with Him there, nothing frightens me, but the slightest diversion away from Him is painful to me.
>
> Spending time in God's presence doesn't weaken the body. Leaving the seemingly innocent and permissible pleasures of the world for a time will, on the contrary, give us comfort. In fact, God won't allow a soul that is searching for Him to be comforted anywhere other than with Him. Hence, it makes sense to sacrifice ourselves for some time in His presence.
>
> This does not mean that you have to suffer in this endeavor. No, God must be served with holy freedom. We should labor

> faithfully, without distress or anxiety, calmly recalling our spirit to God whenever it is distracted.[26]

The great football coach Vince Lombardi was known to say, "Winning isn't a sometimes thing; it's an all the time thing." So it is with the secret place.

3. The secret place is…a secret. "He who dwells in the *secret* place of the Most High." *Secret* means just between us and God. The temptation is terrific to turn the inner sanctum into a show or a profit center. This is what the Pharisees did, and Jesus's grave condemnation made it clear that whatever tangential benefit they were deriving from their freak-show devotion was the only benefit they were going to get. That's why Jesus, man for the people though he was, constantly sought solitude when he wanted to connect with the Father. It's why my mom has risen at four in the morning as long as I've been alive.

4. The secret place is God's place. "He who dwells in the secret place *of the Most High* shall abide under the shadow of the Almighty." We live in a customized culture, and nothing typifies this more than Starbucks. It's fabulously entertaining to stand in line watching people make ten or twelve decisions about one cup of coffee. Indeed, you could say a double tall, skinny, half-caff, two-pump, no-whip, black and white mocha is an icon of our age. Twenty-first-century Americans customize everything. You can have your Whopper your way, design your own Dell computer, even create your personalized bachelor's degree online, however you like it. Saturated as we can become with ourselves and our unique preferences, it's easy to approach our intimate relationship with God like a keen consumer. We have My Yahoo! so why shouldn't we have My Secret Place?

Paul exhorts us to "run in such a way as to get the prize."[27] If we are going to seek God, we are wise to do it on his terms. All the people Jesus said will say to him on that day, "Lord, Lord…" were seeking God. They were running the race; they just weren't running in such a way as to get the prize. If we're going to play, let's play to win. Let's play by the rules made by the one who made us.

So what does that mean? When we seek, pray to, and worship the God of the ages, we need a plumb line. Lots of us read *Could You Not Tarry One Hour?* when we were younger, followed a rather…um… stringent quiet-time format for many years, and one day came to a breakthrough understanding of what it means to be free in Christ. Our well-intentioned self-correction got us free from legalism, but many of us swung too far in the opposite direction, and we grew a little sloppy in our pursuit of the things of God. We have an objective standard for seeking God, and it is the Bible. Psalm 100:4 instructs, "Enter his gates with thanksgiving and his courts with praise; give thanks to him and praise his name." So I often begin my prayer times thanking him for my many blessings. I imagine passing through God's gates and coming onto his property with thankfulness, and then praising my way into the room where he is. Psalm 103:1 says, "Praise the LORD, O my soul; all my inmost being, praise his holy name." So I concentrate on aligning my entire being—heart, mind, body, and spirit—to praise God. Psalm 95:6 reads, "Come, let us bow down in worship, let us kneel before the LORD our Maker." So I often spend time kneeling before the Lord in humble submission. In Psalm 46:10, God directs us to "be still, and know that I am God; I will be exalted among the nations, I will be exalted in the earth." So I'm attentive to spend some time quietly meditating on God's supremacy. Paul aptly summarized this process, encouraging the fledgling believers in Ephesus to "find out what pleases the Lord."[28]

■ ■ ■

In his classic work *The Pursuit of God,* A. W. Tozer wrote:

> Among the famous sayings of the church fathers, none is better known than Augustine's quotation, "Thou hast formed us for Thyself, and our hearts are restless till they find rest in Thee."
>
> The great saint states here in few words the origin and interior history of the human race. God made us for himself—this is the only explanation that satisfies the heart of a thinking man, whatever his wild reason may say. Should faulty education and perverse reasoning lead a man to conclude otherwise, there is little that any Christian can do for him. For such a man, I have no message. My appeal is addressed to those who have been previously taught in secret by the wisdom of God. I speak to thirsty hearts whose longings have been wakened by the touch of God within them, and such as they need no reasoned proof. Their restless hearts furnish all the proof they need.[29]

David had just such a thirsty heart. Before his anointing, before his palace employ, before his exile, and before his ascension, the young shepherd's longings were awakened by the Father's touch. During his young, carefree years, David let himself be taught in secret by the wisdom of God, and when the time of David's calling finally arrived, the pursuit of God's intimate presence was an established norm. That he was made primarily for abiding friendship with the Almighty was a foregone conclusion. This reality drove David to know God in the secret place, a preoccupation that catapulted his calling even as it captivated his heart.

Epilogue

Don't Leave Dagobah Too Soon

> This one a long time have I watched. All his life has he looked away—to the future, to the horizon. Never his mind on where he was.
>
> —YODA, from *The Empire Strikes Back*

Of all the scenes in all the *Star Wars* movies, none is more dispiriting than the scene in which Luke decides to leave the swamp planet of Dagobah. The Empire was striking back, the rebel base on the ice planet Hoth was a pile of rubble, the ragged band of freedom fighters was running scared, Lando was selling out Leia and company in the cloud city, and Han was about to get frozen. Things couldn't have been worse.

During all of this, Luke was in the swamp trying to concentrate on his training. Under the tutelage of the sagacious and sassy Jedi master Yoda, the farm boy from Tatooine was becoming the warrior who would vanquish the evil Imperial forces and restore freedom to the galaxy. (Of course, accepting Luke's metamorphosis required as much willing suspension of disbelief as accepting the Karate Kid's—it's hard to comprehend how Luke got poised and lethal by mounting Yoda's shoulders and swinging from vines. But you still found your heart wrapped around him because you wanted him to grow up and get the goods to beat Darth Vader.)

Then sometime in the middle of his training, the eager pupil's burgeoning Jedi instinct informed him that his friends were in trouble. They had been captured by Vader's forces and their lives were in jeopardy. The resistance movement was hanging by a thread, battle seemed imminent, and Luke was standing on his head balancing rocks. He had a decision to make: *Do I stay in Dagobah and finish my training, or do I pull out and jump into the battle now, when the situation seems so critical?*

My own moment of decision didn't happen while I was standing on my head balancing rocks. It happened halfway through my army commitment when I discovered a way to bail out early. A memo circulated through the junior-officer ranks offering voluntary early separation from active duty in exchange for an increased reserve commitment. My heart leaped when I read the message—I could go free, turn the ship around, and pursue my calling at last! What a glad stroke of fortune, what a serendipitous divine intervention!

It wasn't that the army was bad. I had a good job, had the respect of my men, and earned a fine salary. My commander was tough and exact, but he was a good man who treated me well, and I was learning a great deal from him. I was living comfortably, putting money away, building friendships, and enjoying the sense of nobility that serving my country and following in my father's footsteps afforded me. I wasn't looking to run from anything.

You could say, rather, that I was looking to run *to* something. I had the sense that the battle I was made for was raging *out there* while I was reading topographic maps with a red-lens flashlight in the cupola of a sixty-ton combat vehicle. So it wasn't what I *was* doing as much as what I *wasn't* doing that ate at my heart those long days out in the field.

I knew that America was in a crucial hour. I knew our culture hung in the balance. I knew the church's ability to influence the direction of the nation was waning with every passing day. Within me burned a desire to serve the people of God—to encourage them and equip them and mobilize them for the battle over our country's purpose. Like Luke, I wanted to jump into the battle not for adventure or personal fulfillment but because I sensed that it was my destiny, and I felt I could genuinely help.

It was true: Ministry was my destiny. I could help. But it wasn't time. I remember my discouragement as I prayed and fasted and asked God's blessing on moving forward into my calling. In truth, I saw that time of prayer as a formality—I considered it obvious what I should do. God surprised me, though, by giving me a strong sense that I was to stay where I was. His word indicated so. The authorities he placed in my life said so. And, finally, the quiet witness of the Holy Spirit in my heart confirmed it.

As I look back over the path of my development, I thank God that I obeyed and didn't leave Dagobah too soon. In the intervening years between that decision and my transition into church work, God's preparation was intense and invaluable. I learned to disciple people. I learned to serve a general. I learned to live in the secret place when all the goosebumps and savor of seeking God's presence had long since gone. And when the time was right, God opened the door for me to shift employment easily, naturally, effortlessly—with my eyes on him.

Desert Training

There is no doubt that a spiritual battle is going on. You do have a role to fill in the ranks of God's forces. But don't fall into the trap of thinking that this raging battle will end in a couple of months. Jesus said that the kingdom of heaven has been forcefully advancing from the days of John the Baptist. He made it clear that the end won't come until the gospel of the kingdom has been proclaimed in every nation. So relax, stay steady, and with all your heart, do everything God has put in front of you. What you are doing right now can be of inestimable value in the battle, if only you'll let it.

David had to make this decision. Having fallen from Saul's favor, the man who would be king found himself living in caves and being hunted by the most powerful army in the world. David's shock and delight must have been profound when Saul happened into the cave where David was hiding. Saul entered alone to…um…answer the call of nature. David must have been thinking, *God orchestrated this! He's heard my cry, remembered his promise, and delivered Saul into my hand. And it's not as if I'm murdering him—it's self-defense. He's hunting me, so he's fair game, right? And, after all, it's all part of God's sovereign plan.*

Imagine the temptation for David to take Saul's life, to pull out early from the training grounds of his desert Dagobah! That was his time to end the suffering, to jump tracks, to start his calling as king. But David knew better because David knew God. He knew that the calling was the path, not the endpoint. David let Saul go because he knew at his core that the desert was part of the training, and the training was part of the call.[1]

Worth Living Into

Luke left Dagobah too soon, and it cost him. The bleak scene at the end of *The Empire Strikes Back* bears witness to his folly—Han was frozen, Darth Vader was in total control, and Luke was one hand lighter and hanging from a weathervane.

Please hear me as I wrap up this book: Your calling is worth living into. God is more interested in the process than in the product, so don't bail on the hard stuff in the name of moving into your calling. The hard stuff is part of the calling. We do a disservice to God and we misunderstand his plan when we view the season we're in as a steppingstone to our calling. It's all training, and it's all the calling. Make a habit of giving your life away every day, and be content for God to open the next door. Promotion is his, not yours. Don't leave Dagobah too soon.

Notes

Chapter 1

1. 1 Peter 2:9, NKJV.

Chapter 2

1. 1 Samuel 16:1.
2. 1 Samuel 16:6-12.
3. 1 Samuel 16:12-13.
4. Mike Post and Stephen Geyer, "Believe It or Not," copyright © 1981.
5. Scripture doesn't indicate whether a royal palace existed during Saul's reign, and several versions refer to Saul's house or residence (see 1 Samuel 19:9). However, in several instances I have opted to use the term *palace* when referring to Saul's residence as well as the place where he ruled.

Chapter 3

1. At times throughout the manuscript, I have used masculine pronouns in my illustrations to avoid cumbersome constructions that might be distracting. In other instances, I've either alternated pronouns or used the inclusive "he or she" where feasible.
2. 1 Samuel 13:5-9.
3. 1 Samuel 13:10-14.
4. 1 Samuel 15:22-23.

Chapter 4

1. See Luke 8:6.
2. Larry Bird, *Drive: The Story of My Life* (New York: Doubleday, 1989), 233-34.

3. See 1 Corinthians 2:14; John 4:24.
4. F. Scott Fitzgerald, *The Great Gatsby* (New York: Simon & Schuster, 1995), 6.

Chapter 5

1. Jeremiah 29:1.
2. Jeremiah 29:4-11.
3. Matthew 25:21.

Chapter 6

1. 1 Samuel 16:15-19.
2. 1 Samuel 16:21-22.
3. 1 Samuel 17:14-15.
4. See Luke 14:26.
5. 1 Samuel 17:15.
6. 2 Corinthians 4:4.
7. Matthew 11:12.
8. Isaiah 9:7.
9. 1 Peter 5:8.
10. Matthew 6:10, KJV.
11. See 2 Timothy 3:12.
12. See Ephesians 5:23.
13. Genesis 2:24; see also Mark 10:7-8.
14. Ephesians 6:3.
15. Ephesians 6:7-8, NLT.
16. 1 Peter 2:18-21.
17. Romans 13:1-2.
18. Acts 15:1-2.
19. Acts 15:19-21.

Chapter 7

1. 1 Samuel 17:4-9.
2. 1 Samuel 17:32-37.
3. 1 Samuel 17:48-50.
4. 1 Samuel 16:14-17.
5. 1 Samuel 16:21-22.

Chapter 8

1. 1 Kings 19:4.
2. 1 Kings 19:9-10.
3. 1 Kings 19:19,21.
4. 2 Kings 3:6-7.
5. 2 Kings 3:11.
6. 2 Kings 3:11.
7. 1 Samuel 16:19-21.
8. 1 Samuel 17:32.
9. Matthew 20:26.

Chapter 9

1. John 6:68.
2. Mark 10:29-30.
3. Mark 8:34-35.
4. 1 Samuel 17:20.
5. 1 Samuel 17:20-24.
6. 1 Samuel 17:32.
7. 1 Samuel 17:45-47.

Chapter 10

1. Romans 3:23-24.

2. 1 Peter 2:9.
3. 2 Corinthians 5:21.
4. 1 John 1:1,5.
5. John 14:9.
6. Luke 11:20.
7. Matthew 5:48.
8. 1 John 1:10.
9. 1 John 2:1.
10. 1 John 3:5-6.
11. Psalm 101:2-4.
12. 1 Corinthians 6:18.
13. 1 Corinthians 10:12-14.
14. 1 Timothy 6:9-11.
15. 2 Timothy 2:22.
16. Matthew 6:13.
17. Mark 14:38.
18. Ephesians 5:11.
19. Psalm 97:10; Proverbs 8:13; Romans 12:9.
20. 1 Corinthians 6:9-10.
21. Philippians 3:8.
22. Psalm 101:2-4.

Chapter 11

1. John 10:10.
2. 1 Peter 5:8-9.
3. James 4:7.
4. 1 John 4:4.
5. Dietrich Bonhoeffer, *The Cost of Discipleship* (New York: Collier, 1949), 45.
6. Mark 10:7-8.

Chapter 12

1. 1 Samuel 17:41-44.
2. 1 Samuel 17:45-47.
3. Colossians 3:16.
4. Matthew 12:35.
5. John 16:33.
6. 1 John 5:4-5.
7. 1 John 4:4.
8. John 1:29,36.
9. John 3:30.
10. Matthew 4:1.
11. Matthew 4:2-11.
12. Hebrews 4:12.
13. Luke 2:46.
14. Psalm 119:11.
15. Proverbs 7:1-3.
16. Robert Hendrickson, *The Facts on File Encyclopedia of Word and Phrase Origins* (New York: Facts on File, 1997).
17. Jeremiah 17:9.
18. Psalm 42:5.
19. Joshua 1:8.

Chapter 13

1. 2 Chronicles 20:7.
2. 1 Samuel 18:5.
3. 1 Samuel 18:6-9.
4. 1 Samuel 18:21.
5. 1 Samuel 18:25.
6. 1 Samuel 18:29.
7. 1 Samuel 23:29.

8. D. R. W. Wood and I. H. Marshall, *New Bible Dictionary,* 2nd ed. (Downers Grove, IL: InterVarsity, 1982), 325.
9. Psalm 63:1-8.
10. Psalm 23:1-6.
11. Psalm 17:15.
12. 1 Samuel 13:14.
13. Psalm 18:4-5.
14. Psalm 18:6-18.
15. Psalm 18:19.
16. Matthew 5:21-22,27-28,38-39,43-44.
17. Matthew 6:5-6.
18. John 17:21, NKJV.
19. Matthew 7:21, NKJV.
20. Matthew 7:22, NKJV.
21. Matthew 7:23, NKJV.
22. Matthew 6:6, NKJV.
23. Matthew 7:7-8, NKJV.
24. Psalm 91:1, NKJV.
25. John 15:4.
26. Brother Lawrence, *The Practice of the Presence of God* (New Kensington, PA: Whitaker House, 1982), 35-36.
27. 1 Corinthians 9:24.
28. Ephesians 5:10.
29. A. W. Tozer, *The Pursuit of God* (Camp Hill, PA: Christian Publications, 1982), 31-32.

Epilogue

1. See 1 Samuel 24.